BARREN GROUNDS

Barren Grounds

Fred "Skip" Pessl

THE STORY OF THE TRAGIC MOFFATT CANOE TRIP

Dartmouth College Press | Hanover, New Hampshire

Dartmouth College Press
An imprint of University Press of New England
www.upne.com

Manufactured in the United States of America
Designed by Mindy Basinger Hill
Typeset in Adobe Caslon Pro

University Press of New England is a member of the Green Press Initiative. The paper used in this book meets their minimum requirement for recycled paper.

Library of Congress Cataloging-in-Publication Data
Pessl, Fred.
Barren grounds: the story of the tragic Moffatt canoe trip / Fred Skip Pessl.
pages cm
ISBN 978-1-61168-533-6 (cloth : alk. paper)—
ISBN 978-1-61168-591-6 (ebook)
1. Canoes and canoeing—Northwest, Canadian.
2. Canoeing accidents—Northwest, Canadian.
3. Northwest, Canadian—Description and travel.
I. Title.
GV776.15.N67P47 2014
797.12209719—dc23 2013049866

5 4 3 2 1

THIS BOOK IS DEDICATED

to the memory of Art Moffatt, 1919–1955, friend, mentor, and pioneer of modern wilderness canoeing; and Peter Franck, 1936–2013, companion and resolute adventurer. Gone too soon!

Travel by canoe is not a necessity, and will nevermore be the most efficient way to get from one region to another, or even from one lake to another . . . anywhere. A canoe trip has become simply a rite of oneness with certain terrain, a diversion of the field, an act performed not because it is necessary but because there is value in the act itself.

John McPhee, the *New Yorker* | APRIL 29, 2013

CONTENTS

PREFACE

JULY 2, 1955: Art Moffatt spider-crawled the gunnels and settled on the stern seat of his gray, heavily laden eighteen-foot Chestnut Peterborough prospector canoe, and with Joe Lanouette, Dartmouth sophomore, in the bow, pushed off into the windy, wave-tossed waters of Black Lake, Saskatchewan, intent on leading his party of six men in three canoes on a great adventure to retrace, without native guides and without outside technical support, the nine-hundred-mile epic journey of J. B. Tyrrell, 1893. Two other canoes followed: a red one with Peter Franck, Harvard student, in the stern and George Grinnell, recently discharged from the U.S. Army; and a green one with Skip Pessl, 1955 Dartmouth graduate, in the stern and Bruce LeFavour, Dartmouth sophomore.

J. B. Tyrrell published the account of his 1893 journey down the Dubawnt drainage in the *Geographical Journal,* November 1894. The article describes the geology and general sources of the region, but also includes more personal remarks on the weather, wildlife, travel conditions, his leadership, and the spirit of the party. Selected quotations from his report are interspersed throughout this narrative where Tyrrell's comments contrast or reinforce the Moffatt party journal entries for the same locations. Tyrrell's travel rate also is noted in this narrative, contrasting with the Moffatt party's much slower northward progress.

The route led northeast through a series of south-flowing lakes, swamps, and connecting streams to the height-of-land between Selwyn and Wholdaia Lakes and then down the huge north-flowing drainage of the Dubawnt River, across the legendary Dubawnt Lake (ice-covered often in late summer) to the Thelon River flowing into Baker Lake and eastward to Chesterfield Inlet and Hudson Bay.

Summer 2013: I am writing now as an eighty-year-old grandfather, reflecting on the youthful prose of the Pessl and Franck Dubawnt journals, reconciling my memories with those entries and trying to put in perspective the comments, critiques, and reviews of the Moffatt expedition that came over these many years from the wilderness canoeing

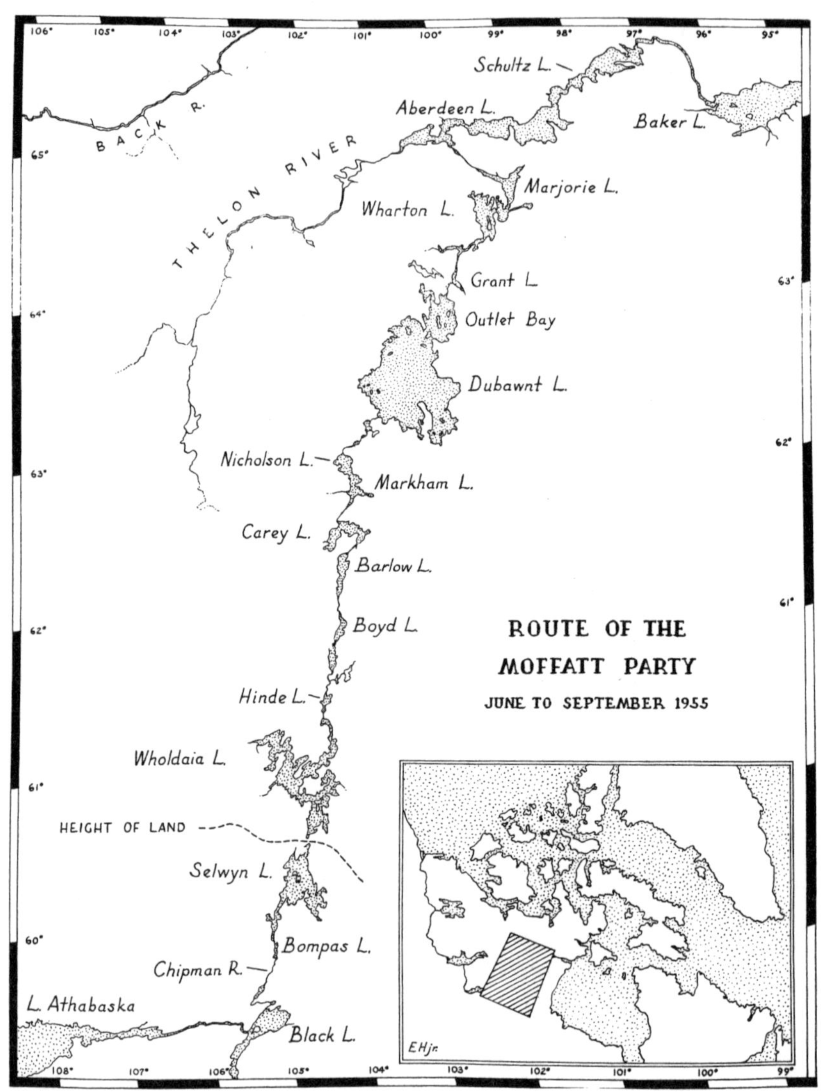

Route of the Moffatt Party by Elmer Harp Jr.

community, many in response to the publication of George Grinnell's account of the journey, *A Death on the Barrens.**

I think the first time I heard about a Dubawnt River canoe journey was in the summer of 1954 on my second Albany River trip with Art. We often talked late in the evening around the campfire embers after the other canoers had left for their tents. He described the history of Tyrrell's journey from Athabasca Lake to Chesterfield Inlet and then down the west coast of Hudson Bay to Churchill, Manitoba. Art had no intention of making the treacherous coastal journey from Chesterfield to Churchill, but he did suggest that if we had time after arriving at the Baker Lake Hudson Bay Company (HBC) post, we might continue on from Baker to Chesterfield Inlet.

A second motivation from Art was the proposal that we make a documentary film using the vehicle of canoe travel to record the change in flora, fauna, and physiography as we traveled from the boreal forests of northern Saskatchewan northeastward along the Dubawnt drainage, through a transition zone of diminishing trees and into a region of true tundra vegetation and wildlife.

I had helped Art on previous Albany River trips to film the canoeing/camping experience that he then used during subsequent winter months to interest and recruit potential young canoers to join him for future summer trips on the Albany River. During those trips, I learned a bit about camera angles, sequenced shots, and background footage. I enjoyed being part of the challenge to record on film at least some of what a wilderness canoe journey was all about, and I understood that this new and much more comprehensive film project was an exciting, demanding priority of the Dubawnt proposal.

I accepted that priority unconditionally, without understanding or contemplating the profound impact the photo priority would have on our travel schedule. I doubt the other party members knew much about the film priority or that it was a major dimension of the trip, even though Art was very specific in his letter of January 27, 1955, to Peter Franck: "I won't be up on the Albany this coming summer. I feel almost certain, because we

**Che-Mun,* Spring 1996.

are planning (Skip Pessl and I) a very long and hard trip north from Lake Athabasca to the Dubawnt River, through the Barrens to Chesterfield Inlet. Nobody has made the trip but one white man and his brother in 1893. From Indian country to Eskimo country. Purpose: another film."

Our group began the trip as an awkward collection of friends and strangers, some having canoed together, others having little or no canoeing experience, and several not even having met each other. Art and I had known each other for four years and had canoed the Albany River twice together. Previously, I made my first canoe trip with my parents on the Manistee River in northwestern Michigan as an eleven-year-old. In subsequent years, we canoed the Michipicoten River–Whitefish Lake drainage in the Algoma country of northern Ontario, the Manuan-Vermillion Rivers, and the Chibougamau-Mistassini Lakes region of southern Quebec. I grew up in the Great Lakes region of southern Michigan, sailing and racing small, one-design boats from nearly as soon as I could walk. Indeed, my nickname was given to me by a Great Lakes ship captain looking through the maternity-ward glass partition at the newborns: "Oh, look at the little skipper." Wind, water, and weather are common elements in sailing and canoeing, and I understood the dynamics of their interactions, although not in the context of wilderness travel on powerful northern drainages.

Art and Peter Franck had canoed the Albany River once together. Joe Lanouette and Bruce LeFavour, college classmates, were young outdoorsmen but with no canoeing experience. Art had met Joe and Bruce early in the winter of 1954–55. I knew none of the party except Art and none of the party had met George Grinnell until he arrived in Stony Rapids on June 27. So we had much "getting to know" during those early days, and unfortunately some differences and tensions were never resolved.

On June 24, I wrote in my journal: "At first glance our party seems to be a good one. Pete is a little young and seems somewhat preoccupied with minor details; still he seems to be a good worker and he has canoeing experience with Art on the Albany. Joe will probably be the problem guy not in terms of personality quirks, but rather in terms of general insensitivity and unconscious selfishness. Hunger, heat, work are viewed

Joe Lanouette on the harmonica in a cold, wet camp.
Courtesy Creigh Moffatt.

as personal affronts and are combated with disregard for his impact on others. But all is not gloom with the Brazilian. He's got a good sense of humor and isn't half bad on the harmonica. Bruce is a hesitating sincere fellow who likes to fish, wants to learn and will always pick up that last lowly job. Grinnell has not appeared as yet."

Some of the tension and controversy that ensued as the trip progressed involved nontravel time devoted to photography, sometimes during fair weather when canoe miles could have been optimized. Art and I were almost exclusively involved in the photography, he with the 16 mm movie camera, I with the 35 mm Leica SLR. The others were involved as subjects when we had camping, river running, or hunting/fishing scenarios, but if we were off filming birds, landscapes, or other general subjects, the guys were hanging around camp wondering about or criticizing the delay in our travel departure. So I think the commitment to filming our Dubawnt journey, whether or not understood and supported by the party members, was a major factor in the negative group dynamics that arose from time to time, especially as the travel season waned and photo delays became more compromising.

Art Moffatt birding along the southwestern shore of Dubawnt Lake. Courtesy Creigh Moffatt.

More importantly, Art and I remained tragically stubborn in our commitment to film the journey, even in the face of serious and obvious deterioration of the weather. Indeed, images of storm-bound campsites with wind-driven snow piled against ragged tents and darkly huddled figures around a smoldering fire pit became a precious part of the story. He was, however, fully aware of the conflict between traveling efficiently and filming the journey. He wrote in his journal on July 31, "but all day reflected on the need to get moving to get out of here before food runs out and storms beset us, and the dilemma of how to make a film of the operation; the two are incompatible."

A few days earlier, on July 18, he had written: "Back and neck and groin tired after yesterday's 1½ mi. portage, but feel fine otherwise. Hope to make good time north from here, but need good weather and must make film."

One afternoon later in the trip when Art and I were out on a photo quest alone, I asked him about our travel schedule, food supply, the weather; I told him we were very close to the bone, that we needed to get out before the country really closed down. I think he understood what

I was saying, but he replied, "Well, but what if we rush to the coast and don't come back with anything?"

But we did gain the height-of-land by working together, gaining in fitness, skills, and confidence, understanding each other's strengths and weaknesses and enjoying the challenges of the journey together.

After seventy-five days of glorious wilderness travel, through lakes and swamps and rivers; at campsites tortured by bugs and others blown free by exposed, windy vistas on to the unbelievable sense of infinity that the Barrens invoke; through the adrenalin rush of finding a canoe path through big waves, crashing currents, and threatening rocks; and into the long-distance mantra of paddling forever on huge lakes of mythic energy and unknown outlets, reality brought us down.

The weather grew harsh. Freezing temperatures, wind-driven snow, dwindling food supplies, and deteriorating equipment pushed us hard to travel faster and more efficiently, and ultimately we made a fatal mistake. We approached the rapids entering Marjorie Lake with caution, but without an onshore look. Standing up in our canoes as we floated toward the rapids, we saw a modest current sweeping toward a right-hand bend and drove our canoes into that initial current V.

The rest is wilderness canoeing history. Two of the three canoes capsized, losing most of the party's food and gear to the river and dumping Art, Joe, Bruce, and Skip in the swirling, frigid waters at the bottom of the rapids and against a small island at the south shore of Marjorie Lake. Art Moffatt died that day.

ACKNOWLEDGMENTS

FROM THE BEGINNING to the end of this project, my most grateful thanks go to my lovely wife, Molly. At the beginning, perhaps as an act of self-defense when faced with a grumpy, bored, post-op housemate, she suggested I take a look at my old Dubawnt journal. "Maybe start transcribing it." From then until now, she has been by my side reading critically, fixing countless computer glitches, creatively making suggestions.

Creigh Moffatt and Daniel Johnson provided access to critical source materials and photographs from the Moffatt family collection, and we have become even closer friends as a result of this project, collaborators and comrades in the quest for historic accuracy.

Fay Franck, Peter's widow, has similarly entrusted me with Peter's journal, early Moffatt correspondence, and photos and news clippings from the family archives. Fay also warmly shared her thoughts and recollections in response to my questions about Peter's interest in the Barrens and his speech patterns. It saddens me that Peter did not live to see this publication nor to appreciate the profound support I received from Fay and the Franck family.

Bruce LeFavour, bowman and tentmate on our Dubawnt journey, contributed importantly to my understanding of Grinnell's United Bowman's Association and its origin and purpose. I am grateful for his quotation.

Walter Bichler of Pfaffstatten, Austria, friend, sailing companion, and photographer extraordinary, reviewed the unedited Moffatt movie film and made single-frame prints from the 16 mm film.

Peter Carini, Dartmouth College archivist, and the Rauner Library staff provided valuable early support in making available Art Moffatt's 1955 trip journal and other related Dubawnt documents.

Many family and friends were avid early readers, and their enthusiasm and curiosity were a sustaining force, most notably Pat Marshall, Andy Seaver, Harry and Amy Beal, Neil and Bonnie Roberts, Andy Gray, the Bay Area, Bozeman, and Seattle Pessls, Bruce Foxworthy, and Vladomir Radojevic.

Al Kesselheim, wilderness paddler, author, friend, and mentor, helped me immensely, not only with the nuts and bolts of writing but with his continuing interest in the Moffatt Dubawnt story, with sharing of his family's wilderness experiences and his special 2012 story about the Moffatt adventure in *Canoe & Kayak* magazine.

Chic Scott, author, backcountry ski companion and Canadian mountaineering historian, read an early draft, and with the frankness of a true friend suggested that my Dubawnt experience was a great adventure story and that I take a narrative writing class. Both suggestions had merit.

Bill Truettner, dear friend and companion, author, and Smithsonian art historian, read an early draft with enthusiasm and helped translate the publisher's contract for me.

More recently, my introduction to the leaders and members of the Wilderness Canoeing Association has opened my awareness of a remarkable subculture of energetic, courageous adventurers who collectively seem to have canoed almost all the navigable waters of North America, each with remarkable stories of excitement, accomplishment, and insight. And in spite of their own amazing experiences, they were so warmly hospitable and sincerely interested in my presentation at the 2013 Wilderness Canoeing Symposium that I am still coasting on the energy and support of that time together. Thank you Marilyn and David Friesen, John Lentz, Fred Gaskin, James Raffan, Mart Gross, David Freeman, Dick Irwin, Ross McIntyre, Al Stirt, and all those many others in that warm and attentive audience.

Of all the people in the wilderness canoeing community, I owe my most heartfelt gratitude to George Luste, wilderness paddler, author, publisher, founder and convener of the Wilderness Canoeing Symposium, and a warm and gracious personal friend. George published the first edition of Grinnell's account of the '55 Dubawnt journey and contributed an informed, thoughtful commentary to that publication. He invited me to the 2013 symposium and effectively countered my initial reluctance. While I was at the symposium in Toronto, he shared his home, his family and his lifelong northern experience with me. I am forever grateful.

And then, Aleks Gusev, paddler, editor, friend, and the driving force behind the *Nastawgan* magazine "Dubawnt Special" issue—which reinforced my belief that Dubawnt adventures, beginning probably before Tyrrell and continuing to this day by modest wilderness travelers—was of interest to many people and worth the effort to tell my Dubawnt story. Thank you, Aleks!

Gloria Campbell has been my most local and immediate advocate. We began a "Dubawnt" relationship nearly a year ago when I was a student in her Nontraditional Publishing college course. Gloria instructed me about the practical world of publishing and offered encouragement, and when I lost most of the manuscript to a computer glitch, she stepped up to retype and format an acceptable product from previous documents that I was able to recover. She has been a partner and mentor from early on.

Richard Pult, my acquisition editor at University Press of New England, is still just a voice and a spirit in the complex process of moving from a draft manuscript to a product on the shelf, but he is a comfortable, supportive, and creative advocate for this Dubawnt project. I look forward to continuing collaboration and maybe even a face-to-face moment. And Richard's UPNE colleagues, David Corey, Barbara Briggs, Katy Grabill, Sherri Strickland, and Lauren Seidman have all endured my innocence as a first-time book author and have helped make the book the best it can be. Copy editor Drew Bryan worked hard to improve clarity and consistency in the text. To all these professionals I appreciate your efforts and I have learned very much.

Certainly an acknowledgment is appropriate, perhaps even a "thank you," to George Grinnell for his 1996 account of his Dubawnt experience. Without that provocation, even with Molly's nudge, I might not have embarked on this Dubawnt project. It has been a very satisfying ride.

Thank you all!

Planning the Trip

SERIOUS PLANNING for the Dubawnt journey began in late fall 1955, when Art Moffatt and I committed to the project and he began the complex process of food and equipment selection and purchasing, something he had done many times for his Albany River trips. Even though the Dubawnt journey would be nearly twice the distance of the Albany River trip and under much more isolated, challenging conditions, meal planning and equipment allocations were familiar chores.

The greater challenge of the Dubawnt project was in the recruitment of experienced, motivated young men, available for the full summer, able to afford the estimated individual expense of $600, and willing to accept nasty bugs, long portages, unpredictable weather, and marathon paddling.

On January 12, Art launched that recruiting effort with a letter to the Dartmouth Outing Club describing the proposed trip and soliciting interest from the Dartmouth community. Shortly thereafter he contacted Peter Franck, Harvard freshman, who had previously canoed the Albany River with Art. Within a week Peter had committed to the project.

By February 4 Art had been informed by his neighbors, Lewis and Virginia Teague, that a young member of their extended family, George Grinnell, soon to be discharged from the U.S. Army, might be available.

Bruce LeFavour and Joe Lanouette attended an illustrated lecture by Art on the Dartmouth campus early in the 1955 academic year. Art described previous canoe trips on the Albany River and at the end of his presentation he announced that he was planning a longer trip, farther north into the Canadian Barrens, and that he needed two more people to complete the party. Bruce recalls, "Joe and I signed up on the spot."

By early May the party members had been identified and most of the procurement and logistical support established. Art sent a news release to the *New York Times* announcing "Six Americans to Cross Canadian Barrens By Canoe."

The following documents exemplify Art's careful, realistic approach to recruitment and expedition planning.

ARTHUR R. MOFFATT **Films** NORWICH, VERMONT

Tel. 787-M1

February 4, 1955

Dear Pete,

I am delighted to hear you'd like to join us this summer on the Dubawnt trip. Although you state in your last letter, I've written to your father to acquaint him with details of the journey, and also to give him some idea of the various risks and uncertainties involved, which I'm afraid I didn't make any too clear in my earlier letter to you.

First (I assume you've looked at a map) the trip is long -- perhaps 800 or 900 miles in all. This means we're going to have to leave as soon as possible -- you probably won't have time to go to California. If we're in Edmonton, Alberta, by June 20 or so, we're still going to have to hustle to get down to Chesterfield Inlet before freezeup, which is often as early as September. If we miss hte last schooner, we're stuck until there's enough ice to land a plane at Chesterfield and Churchill.

There are no posts between Athabaska and Baker Lake, just above Chesterfield Inlet. We're going to have to pack enough food for four men for three months in the two canoes -- if you thought we ate badly on the Albany, wait'll you hit the Dubawnt. It'll be good old oatmeal, hardtack, macaroni, and bully beef till it's coming out of our ears.

We do have permission to carry rifles to hunt caribou, but we can hunt only if starvation threatens. And in case of accident, loss of a canoe, or the like, starvation would definitely threaten in a very short time in that country. The herds of caribou are supposed to be numberless on the barrens in summer, but they are not necessarily going to be thick or even present at any given point where we happen to have our postulated disaster.

Fish abound -- trout up to 25 pounds.

So do flies and mosquitoes -- in hordes twenty times

PAGE 1

Letter from Art Moffatt to Peter Franck.
Courtesy Fay Franck.

worse than anything we saw on the Albany.

The portages are tough, especially the first half dozen out of Athabaska Lake, just when we still have all our food to pack. Two and three miles long, and through muskeg -- like Speckled Trout, I gather.

Dubawnt Lake, fifty miles across, is frozen all summer long. The ice leaves the west shore open when the wind blows from the west -- otherwise the ice piles up on shore, when the wind is from the east. We will probably have to wait, probably portage some of the way, and in general have very rough going at this point.

Wood, of course, will be absent for more than half the trip, which means that there will be no fires for cooking or warmth except when we can gather enough dry willows or moss -- or if we take the trouble to pack a primus stove and gas to burn in it.

I guess that covers the difficulties and dangers. New to all of us will be the Chipwyan Indians around Athabaska, the Barren Grounds themselves, the Caribou, the Inland, or Caribou Eskimos, and the very long days -- 20 to 22 hours of sunlight.

If you want to read up on any of this in your spare time I would suggest Tyrrell's "Across the Sub-Arctics of Canada", the story of the only other party to make the trip; Farley Mowatt's "People of the Deer"; Volume V of the Report on the 5th Thule Expedition; also Volumes VI and VII. All should be available in your library down there. Read them with map at hand.

Finally, as to costs: it is likely that we will run into unexpected expenses, but to start with I feel that $600 ought to cover the trip from Toronto to Winnipeg. As I said earlier in my other letter, we're each chipping in that amount, and if there is any left when we get back to Winnipeg, we'll divide it equally. If not, we may each need to chip in a little more. The trip is not one of my regular Hudson Bay Trips, and each of us will be travelling at his own risk. As the oldest and most experienced, I'll do the organizing and make the decisions, Skip will be 2nd in Command.

We're going to have two brand new 18 foot Chestnuts for canoes, possibly new tents, and I'll supply the packsacks, cooking gear, and so on.

PAGE 2

If you continue on with the 150 Pound Crew you should be in top shape for the trip -- and you'll xxt stay that way through the summer, paddling and portaging.

It will probably be a week or so before I hear from your father, but as soon as I do I'll let you know, and in the meanwhile you can be thinking it all over once again, reading up on it if you have the time.

I hope you still like the idea as much now that you know more about what we'll face, and I look forward to seeing it all settled that you will be with us.

Incidentally, the fourth member of the party may by a lad named Grinnell, about 22, left Harvard after his Freshman year for the Marines, and is getting out this May. His grandfather founded the Audubon Society, I believe. That would make the trip a sort of Harvard-Dartmouth Expedition. But this is not definite.

As far as coming up here goes, you are welcome anytime, but unless you have a lot of questions, things have not yet jelled enough to make a visit worthwhile. When the whole thing is settled, re personnell and so on, I'd like to get everybody together up here for an organizational meeting -- say in March or early April.

I can't recall now whether I told you that I've been down your way fairly often with my film this winter -- Waltham Women's Club, General Electric Plant in Lynn, Brooks Club of New Bedford, White Fund Course in Lawrence, and so on. So your question about the moom pitchur business is answered in a word - good.

All the best, then --

Art

P.S. Have you a more precise address than the one on the envelope of this letter? If so, shoot it along.

PAGE 3

April 29, 1955

Dear Pete,

This is to give an account of our expenses per man this summer, and to let you see how much more money you will need for personal and miscellaneous expenses.

Fare, White River Jct., Vt. - Toronto	$25.00
" Toronto-Prince Albert, Sask.	50.90
Berth, " " "	8.00
Plane Fare, Prince Albert - Stony Raps	59.00
Meals from WRJ - Stony Raps (approx)	30.00
1/2 share one canoe	92.65
Food on trip per man	100.00
Total spent reaching Baker Lake	365.55
Fare - Churchill - Winnipeg	39.15
Fare - Winnipeg - Toronto	34.75
Berth - Churchill - Winnipeg	8.75
Berth - Winnipeg - Toronto	5.85
Meals - Churchill-Toronto (approx)	25.00
Fare - Hanover - Toronto	25.00
Freight on canoes - Edmonton - Stony Raps	15.00
	153.50
plus Hanover-Baker Lake	365.55
Total	519.05

You will note that the plane fare from Baker Lake to Churchill is not included. This will be at least $50 and may be $100. In any case, the $600 per man will be entirely used up before we get home.

In your case, you will also have to get up here fro[m] Cambridge, and back there again in the fall. I want

PAGE I

Letter from Art Moffatt detailing expenses.
Courtesy Fay Franck.

to point out that we have figured very close to the line, and that a few days of unexpected delay between trains or planes, etc, with attendant hotel and food bills, would put a severe strain on our finances.

Also, there is no provision for a geiger counter, for personal gear, or personal expenses -- tobacco, candy, moccasins, parkas, or what have you.

I would suggest, therefore, that after completing all your purchases for equipment, and after obtaining your ticket from Cambridge to Hanover (White River Junction), you still have at least $100 in cash with you, for use in any emergency or for possible personal expenditures. More than this, if possible, would be good insurance.

Traveler's Cheques would be the best way to carry such funds. If you buy them in Toronto, between trains, you would have them in easily negotiable Canadian funds.

The canoes have been shipped and are paid for. In addition, a deposit of $150 has been sent to the HBC toward our supplies at Stony Rapids.

You have already contributed $300 toward our bulk funds, and the rest, another $300, will be welcome at any time. I will have to convert this bulk fund into Canadian dollars here before we leave, so the sooner we get this done the better.

As soon as I have all the loose ends of information on trains, planes, etc., I'll let you know final costs of the plane from Baker Lake to Churchill, and our definite time schedule of departure.

All the best,

PAGE 2

NEWS RELEASE

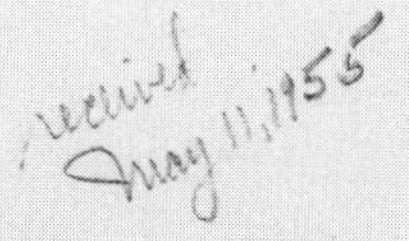

From: A. R. Moffatt
Norwich, Vermont
Tel. Norwich 787-M1

SIX AMERICANS TO CROSS CANADIAN BARREN GROUNDS BY CANOE

Former Long Island man will lead party of college men over 900 mile route untraveled since 1893.

New York, May 12--

An American canoeman is in town today completing plans for his trip this summer across the Northwest Territories of Canada, the last and biggest wilderness area on continental North America.

He is Arthur R. Moffatt, 36 years old, of Norwich, Vermont, who was born in Syosset, L.I., and spent the first twenty years of his life in this area. In 1937, while still living in Syosset, he made his first long canoe trip, starting out alone in an 18 foot canoe from Sioux Lookout, Ontario, and paddling northeast 700 miles along the Albany River to James Bay, the southern part of Hudson Bay.

His goal this summer is once again Hudson Bay, but he plans to begin his trip at Stony Rapids, on Lake Athabaska in northern Ssskatchewan, and travel north via the Dubawnt River to Chesterfield Inlet on Hudson Bay, two hundred miles south of the Arctic Circle.

This route was first traveled by Dr. J. B. Tyrrell, of the Canadian Geological Survey, who with his brother and six Indians surveyed the route in 1893. Since that time, no other white men

PAGE I

News release from Art Moffatt detailing the expedition. Courtesy Creigh Moffatt.

have made the trip, which lies for the most part in completely uninhabited country.

Dr. Tyrrell, who is now 94 years old and lives in Toronto, Ontario, has written Mr. Moffatt to wish him the best of luck and to inform him that he will be travelling on a bad river, in very inhospitable country, and that unless plenty of supplies are carried, starvation will threaten from very early in the trip.

Since this will be his seventh canoe trip to Hudson Bay, Mr. Moffatt feels equal to the task. And he feels that the men he has chosen to accompany him are the right kind to have along--two of them have already been with him on previous trips.

Three of the students with Mr. Moffatt are from Dartmouth College. They are Fred Pessl , Jr., class of '55, from Grosse Pointe Woods, Michigan, who has made two trips to Hudson Bay; Edward Lanouette, class of '57 from Sao Paulo, Brazil; and Bruce LeFavour, class of '57, from Amsterdam, New York.

One man is from Harvard, class of '58. He is Peter Franck, from San Mateo, California, a veteran of one trip to Hudson Bay with Mr. Moffatt.

The last member of the trip is George Grinnell, 57 East 80th Street, New York City, a grand-nephew of George Bird Grinnell, famous explorer, anthropologist, and author.

The hazards and difficulties of a trip down the Dubawnt River are many: The 50 mile expanse of Dubawnt Lake, about half-way to Chesterfield Inlet, was almost completely frozen over when reached by the Tyrrell party in mid-August of 1893, and it will probably be frozen this summer. There are many dangerous rapids

PAGE 2

Page 3 A. R. Moffatt
Norwich, Vermont

in the river, and long portages around the worst of them. Most of the route lies out on the barren tundra, where there will be no wood for fires. And finally, the problem of how to carry enough food for six men for three months is acute--for although the Canadian Government is permitting the party to carry rifles, these may not be used unless starvation threatens.

Reaching Hudson Bay will not solve all problems for the party. The nearest railroad is at Churchill, Manitoba, 400 miles to the south. To reach this point by canoe before freeze-up is out of the question, and since all boats will have left Chesterfield Inlet before the party gets there in early September, the only alternative is to fly out. But thin ice forms in Chesterfield Inlet in mid-September, and this would prevent planes equipped with pontoons from landing. The party might have to wait until ice has formed that is thick enough to support planes equipped with skis.

As head of the expedition, Mr. Moffatt has these objectives in mind:

1. To reach Hudson Bay at Chesterfield Inlet.
2. To produce a color film of the trip, showing the northward progression from Indians and trees to barren tundra and Eskimos.
3. To make notes on the Archaeology and ornithology of the region.
4. To gather material for a book.

Behind him at his 150 year old farmhouse in Vermont, Mr. Moffatt will leave his wife Carol, also a former Long Islander, who accompanied him on a trip to Hudson Bay in 1948; his daughters

Page 4 A. R. Moffatt

Norwich, Vermont

Creigh, 4 years old, and Deborah, 2 years old.

The party is privately financed, and except for camera equipment, only the simplest camping and travelling gear will be taken along.

"Although we can't hunt," Moffatt says, "we will be travelling much as the Indians used to--paddling all the way. It will be a hard trip in many ways. The lack of wood for fires, the flies and mosquitoes, the weather--Tyrrell reported snow storms in late August--will make things uncomfortable, to say the least."

###

PAGE 4

HUDSON BAY TRIPS
ARTHUR R. MOFFATT, DIRECTOR
NORWICH, VERMONT

May 23, 1955

Mr. Thomas G. Franck
320 California Street
San Francisco 4, California

Dear Mr. Franck:

It is now definite that we will be leaving here on June 16 for the Northwest Territories, reaching Stony Rapids on Athabaska Lake on Monday, June 20. Our canoes will arrive at that point on June 24, by which time we should have all our supplies bought and packed.

A few details have been changed: Skip Pessl will travel with us from Toronto, leaving George Grinnell, the member of the party in the army, to catch us by plane and to check with us should anything be missing at Stony Rapids.

We have had to give up the idea of taking a radio transmitting and receiving set north. The Canadian Government has permitted us many things, but this is not to be one of them. They will not license us to take the equipment, even though they recognize the increase in safety such a set would give our party. I have tried several avenues of approach in connection with this radio, and none have proved fruitful.

Finally, I have recently sent Peter the letter a copy of which I enclose. Today I have at last heard from the airline "Arctic Wings", Churchill, Manitoba, which informs me that we will be able to radio for a plane when we reach Hudson Bay, and that the cost for the plane trip out will be a little under $1200 if we use a DC-3, which can carry all our equipment, or $900 if we use a float-equipped Norseman, which might necessitate our leaving part of the gear behind. $200 per man.

I received this information with mixed feelings, since it assures the men who must get back to college a way home on time, but the cost of the plane trip is much higher than I anticipated. We have to pay for the plane both going and coming.

As you will note from the account in my letter to Peter,

PAGE I

Letter from Art Moffatt to Peter Franck's father, Thomas. Courtesy Fay Franck.

all our basic expenses save this plane trip from Baker Lake to Churchill are nicely covered by the $600. In accordance with your suggestion in a recent letter, I think you should know that Peter's expenses are apparently going to run closer to $800 than to $600, and that he should have about that amount at his disposal.

There is still the possibility that we may find some other means of reaching Churchill inexpensively and on time, by boat or by plane (I have been informed that a large scale military installation is being put in at Chesterfield Inlet) and that once on the spot we can arrange such transport. But it will not do to count on it.

Therefore, if you feel that the amount required is not out of the question, I hope you will see that Peter is adequately financed.

If you do feel it is too much money, I would not blame you asking Peter to give up the trip, even at this late date. It was my optimistic belief that we could get out via schooner (which may yet turn out to be true) that caused the problem.

Should Peter be allowed to continue with his plans, he will come up here about June 14 for the check on his equipment by me, stay with us a day or two, and we will start together from White River Junction.

My best regards to you and Mrs. Franck.

Sincerely,

Arthur R. Moffatt

Arthur R. Moffatt

PAGE 2

The Journals

GETTING STARTED

TYRRELL, 1893	LOCATION	MOFFATT, 1955
July 7	Black Lake (departure)	July 2
July 16	Selwyn Lake	July 12–16

Skip | JUNE 21, PRINCE ALBERT

After three days of grimy, restless train travel, our party arrived in Prince Albert, Saskatchewan and spent the night in the Marlburo Hotel. The next morning, we flew north to Stony Rapids at the eastern end of Athabasca Lake, touching down briefly at Lac LaRonge. Stony is much more extensive than the Albany River posts. The Indians often speak English and seem generally to be in better physical shape. But for us, the "semi-roughing it" of a dirty cabin, borrowed utensils and the dusty boredom of an outpost camp is a depressing way to begin a trip; it will only really begin when we have left Stony and start north.

Today the Indian Agency pays treaty money to the Indians. Five dollars per head " . . . God save the Queen!"

Skip | JUNE 24, STONY RAPIDS

Three days of boredom diverted somewhat by reading, busywork, swimming and cooking. Food supplies which didn't arrive on the HBC boat have been replaced with supplies from HBC here at Stony. Most of the original order has been filled. Greater part of today was spent in packing the food and equipment. We are carrying almost 1000 lbs. of grub, much of which is stored in wooden boxes—tumplines are in order. The first portage looms ahead as a swampy, 2½-mile, ordeal. It's interesting how the unpleasantness of this first exertion pervades our minds and seems to hold us back in spite of our eagerness to get underway.

Spent a good bit of time building boxes, sheaths, and mending chores; my personal enjoyment of puttering is getting a good workout.

At first glance, our party seems to be a good one. Pete is a little young and seems somewhat preoccupied with minor details; still, he seems to be a good worker. And he has canoeing experience with Art on the Albany. Joe will probably be the problem guy, not in terms of personality quirks, but rather in terms of general insensitivity and unconscious selfishness. Hunger, heat, work are viewed as personal affronts and are combated with disregard for his impact on others. But all is not gloom with the Brazilian. He's got a good sense of humor and isn't half bad on the harmonica. Bruce is a hesitating, sincere fellow who likes to fish, wants to learn and will always pick up that last lowly job. Grinnell has not appeared as yet.

Forest fires in the northwest send clouds of smoke over the entire horizon; Indians drafted to fight same. Beard grows longer, blacker and more bothersome; bugs less noticeable and solitary tooth brushing more wistful.

Skip | JUNE 25, STONY RAPIDS

Regular Huck Finnish sort of day. We left camp about eleven, paddled down the Fon du Lac River for an hour or so in bright morning sun; found a beautiful sand beach on the south shore of Stony Lake; reminded me of an ideal South Pacific island: long sloping beach edged with thinned-out birch clusters, beautiful flowering ground cover, cool, no flies . . . lunch, snooze, swimming. Bruce and I then spent an hour trolling . . . one jackfish. More swimming and then a hard upstream paddle right into a steaming pot of glop.

Visited by Fred, one-eyed Indian. He's looking for a job and seems very insistent on coming with us. No soap.

First treat of paddling today . . . sore arms, sunburn and a renewal of the slow, psychological tempo of the canoe.

Peter | JUNE 25, STONY RAPIDS

Last night I went to the dance alone early. A lot of Indian girls and a few white boys from Canadian Nickel, all liquored up, swinging around and having a good time. They played round dances at first (school teacher on accordion) and I danced a lot, but when the school teacher quit and they struck up square dances on the fiddle, I sat the rest of the night out with all the rest, except Skip. I love to listen to the fiddle. The dancing was just a lot of running around.

On Saturday, we all, except Art, got in the canoes and went down river quite a ways, about 7 mi. We found a fine sand bank, had lunch and a swim; clear sky and hot sun; a really beautiful day. My new paddle warped all over the place, so it is easier to paddle on one side of the blade than on the other. My right shoulder began to get pretty tired and ache, but that is the only part of me that got tired. I didn't have too much trouble throwing the canoe on my shoulder and carrying it, and I found that I could still paddle stern pretty well.

Glop

Fill pot ¾ full of water and place over fire

To the cold water add:

- 1 can dehy. Veggies
- 2 lg. chopped onions
- 3 cans bully beef or spam or caribou, fish . . .
- 3 cubes bouillon

When water boils, add 2 lbs. macaroni.

Cook until macaroni is soft.

Remove from fire and add:

- 1 can tomato paste

Season with salt, pepper, sage curry . . .

Add flour in cold paste if thickening is desired

Return pot to fire and warm with constant stirring until ready to eat

This may vary with the condition of the larder; chopped cheese added with seasoning and allowed to partially melt is tops; extra veggies also help.

Eat & Sink!

After lunch we went still further and then came back against the current, a tough haul on no previous practice. The right shoulder got pretty sore. When we got back to the shack, it was terribly hot with the stove going full blast and Art cooking glop. I drank too much water and ate two and-one-half bowls of glop, so full that I could hardly move. Then I doused down tea and pudding, plus a can of plums later on. Henry, the old Indian, came up and started telling about old times again and we got the same old story about how bad the portages are, probably true.

Skip | JUNE 26, STONY RAPIDS

Art and I spent a very worthwhile Sunday photographing the Indians at Stony Lake. Walked over to the village with Scotty Johnstone, the HBC manager, around 10 AM and began the film sequence with a short approach shot into the village; individual scenes followed: dogs, kids swimming, father giving son a haircut, tribal chief, toboggan; and ended with Father Peron and farewell. We enjoyed lunch of coffee, biscuits and butter with the school teacher, Mr. Babbin and his wife. It seems that the biggest problem for this very sincere teacher is to persuade the children to wear bathing suits. So far, the attempt degenerates into a ragged strip of cloth tied very sheepishly around the waist. The kids look more embarrassed and very much more naked with this adornment of morality.

I made a rather expensive bargain with Louis Chicken, Chief of the Stony Lake Indians, for his moccasins today. They are a bit different from the Albany counterpart, with more beadwork and no fur trim. The men seem to have very small feet here and I hope that my hesitating estimate of Dana's* delicate pinkies is realistic. It'll make a fine story if all goes well: "bought right off the feet of an honest to goodness Indian Chief . . . Ho-Boy!"

Skip | JUNE 27, STONY RAPIDS

Today the eagerly awaited plane arrived with George Grinnell aboard, completing our party of six. George will be a valuable addition to our

*Dana Darwin, Smith College, girlfriend.

group; seems like an intelligent guy, full of pep and curiosity who was unwilling to meet the structure of college life. New York sophistication combines with a two-year hitch in the Army to bring us a practical, witty, strong guy, albeit an inexperienced canoeist.

The additional supplies we ordered from Prince Albert were not on this plane and we are now faced with the alternative of a week-long additional wait or proceeding with makeshift supplies . . . leaning toward the latter.

Spent an enjoyable evening with Grace Wyat, the nurse at Stony. She is an English woman who has spent most of her career in India and Southeast Asia and walked out of Burma during the Japanese advance in '43. Her family album was a pleasant surprise of interesting snaps of the Indian and Burmese people and their country. There is so much of this world to see and experience and so many cultures which all seem to have a way to happiness that it would be a tragic mistake to miss out and ignore the fascination and value of more travel experiences, however they might happen.

Louis Chicken seems to have misunderstood the moccasin deal. All he could say was, "Too small, too small." Better luck tomorrow.

Skip | JUNE 28, STONY RAPIDS

Completed the moccasin deal with Louis Chicken this morning!

Day was spent packing the remaining supplies in every conceivable container we had available . . . boxes, cartons, crates, duffle bags, tarpaulins, paper sacks; and then the fearsome anxiety of an initial loading to estimate a canoe load. The little "birch bark" practically disappears under the pile of supplies; but finally, after much pushing, shoving and cursing, the canoe was loaded with ⅓ of the total provisions; unloaded again, and then back to the shack for the usual evening of glop, mosquitoes and Henry.

Henry Lafferty is a talkative old guy who seems to have spent a good part of his younger life trapping and fishing in the country north of Stony; maybe actually as far north as the Barrens, maybe not, but he has plenty of stories of a harsh country with severe storms anytime, all summer long, and terrible rapids stretching for miles through steep, inescapable, rocky canyons. He's been visiting our camp for the past few evenings and his stories just seem to make our journey more challenging and more exciting.

Haul road from Stony Rapids to Black Lake put-in, through dense, mixed growth of jack pine, spruce, poplar, white birch, and tamarack; wildfire smoke in the distance. Courtesy Creigh Moffatt.

Rain threatened the entire day and the intense heat of the past few days made the prospect of a cooling shower very welcome . . . but no luck, the black curling thunder clouds blew over.

Skip | JUNE 29, BLACK LAKE

Rose early this morning, 7 AM, cooked breakfast for the guys (hell of a time activating Art) and were loading Tralenberg's truck by 9 AM. One sweaty hour later we're all set; handshakes, goodbyes, last minute purchases, and then up into the truck, 4 in the bed, 2 in the cab. Fifteen miles to Black Lake through dry, sandy, spruce-covered ridges which seem to be the trademark of this country. At about the ten-mile mark, a beautiful and scary mushroom cloud appeared to the north. After this first cloud, five or six similar billows became visible on the horizon. Forest fires seemed to be dotted throughout the entire country, each producing a bulbous cloud resembling a miniature atomic burst.

For the first time since leaving Detroit, I have the feeling that the real trip has finally begun. In spite of the rather dismal setback of leaving our extra paddles in Stony and the delay of awaiting their arrival, we are in our tents on a quiet, rocky point; the smell of cooking and an open fire still lingers with the dying sun. The far bank is bathed in the ruby light of twilight, and perhaps the most valuable feeling of all . . . the peaceful independence I feel when the rest of the world is left behind and solitude becomes an intense, mystical enthusiasm.

Peter | JUNE 29, BLACK LAKE

We finally got underway about 10:30 this morning. It took us quite a while to load all of our stuff on the truck. Tralenberg sat around and gave us helpful advice. One gem was that our packs were too big and heavy for the portages: we should make them lighter, as if we hadn't been worrying about this all along. Finally, we got the three canoes piled on top and took off. The truck was overloaded, about five hundred pounds, and the road was pretty bumpy. God knows how we managed to get to Black Lake. On the way over, we noticed a huge pillar of smoke that kept getting bigger. By the time that we got to Black Lake, it was enormous. We got everything unloaded and packed into the canoes and all were ready to shove off, when we found that we had no spare paddles, just one per man. It would be ridiculous to start on a long, dangerous trip with no spare paddles so there was nothing to do but send a message back through Tralenberg and wait for the next car to bring them, so we paddled about one-half mile away from Camp Grayling at the end of the road around the point so as to be out of sight, and we camped there on a big rock shelf, fairly free of mosquitoes. Everyone felt pretty happy to be outside and away from Stony, even though we were still not really on our way. The lake water was surprisingly warm and everyone had a swim, except Art who hardly ever goes in the water. The whole sky was overcast with smoke so that the sun was only a dim orange ball. George is my bow man, sleeping in the same tent with me. God help me on the snoring. He doesn't seem too cooperative and sort of lazy and critical, but I hope that we work together well soon. I always rub people the wrong way.

Skip | JUNE 30, BLACK LAKE

Spent the entire day here at Black Lake looking for little odd jobs to somehow pass the time; mending, sewing, repairing . . . anything. The early part of the day we had to wait for the three extra paddles we had left behind at Stony Rapids. Tralenberg brought them over on his next trip, arriving about 2:30 PM. However, the wind began to freshen around noon and by 3:00 PM when we would have been able to travel the remaining 12 miles to the Black Lake portage, the waves were running 2–3 ft high, making it impossible to travel with our loaded canoes. So here we are for another night, hoping for fair skies tomorrow. In retrospect, it almost seems as if our party is destined not to complete this trip. After what seems to be a good start we seem to be inevitably plagued by some sort of mishap or unfortunate circumstance. Much of this delay however is due to our lingering between village society and the bush. Once we complete the Black Lake portage and are completely on our own things should straighten out. Beard no longer itches.

Peter | JUNE 30, BLACK LAKE

We sat around waiting for the paddles. Bruce and I decided to paddle down to the rapids and fish for grayling and we left about 8:30. No one was up when we got to Camp Grayling, so we left the canoe there and walked down one side. Bruce stopped at one hole near the upper end and I got going for about a mile and one-half, fishing a little when I saw a good spot and bush-whacking most of the way. I never got a single strike, but that was probably because I was fishing badly. There wasn't enough room for a back cast, so I couldn't get my line out properly. I was contented just to watch the river as it rushed through its narrow channel. The last rapid I came to was enormous. The river narrowed down and dropped eight feet all at once. There was so much water pouring through that it made that little drop seem like Niagara Falls. After looking at this for a while, I came back up and found Bruce in the same spot. We went back to Camp Grayling to find out about the paddles. Someone had taken them up last night and left them at an Indian mission, 2 miles further on. They said they would bring them to our camp.

We got back in time for lunch and sat around reading and sleeping 'til dinner. After dinner, I sat out along the shore alone to look at the lake. The wind was blowing very hard and big waves were crashing into the shore. The shore was mostly rocky cliffs with an occasional bay and sandy beach. Art and George joined me as I was watching the waves. I walked on with them until we found a little park in the trees. It reminded me of some of the Alpine meadows of the Sierras. The trees were large and far apart and there was no undergrowth or grass, just lichens underfoot. Then I started back alone. I still don't talk to George out of shyness.

Skip | JULY 1, BLACK LAKE

Wind-bound the entire day. Blowing from the east; 3–4-ft waves; finally dying in the evening; prospects good for traveling tomorrow. The sky has been filled with smoke from nearby fires; occasionally, the blue sky above the smoke peeks through, emphasizing the murky, dustiness of the day. Took a long walk this morning. Spent a while rock climbing; playing riverboat man on an old barge; following old winter portages; goosing willow ptarmigans. Found a fine set of caribou antlers which I hope will find their way to home. Up at six tomorrow, so good night. Jody's wedding!*

Peter | JULY 1, BLACK LAKE

We were wind-bound here, so we spent the day just sitting and waiting for the waves to go down, which never happened. I read Steinbeck's "To a God Unknown." Once I get started in a novel that I like, I can't put it down until I am finished.

The glop is getting very tasteless without the tomato paste and with macaroni every God damn night.

I am still the same way toward George. He seems very friendly with Skip, but often sits alone looking into the distance for long hours. I don't know what to make of him. Bruce, Joe and I took a canoe and went to a

*Joe D. Mathewson, Dartmouth classmate.

good spot for lake trout and Bruce caught two around 4½ lb. I was trolling a smaller Dare Devil, but never got so much as a nibble.

Skip | JULY 2, 1955, BLACK LAKE

Morning found us enthusiastically preparing for our departure. Breakfast at 7 AM; away before 10 AM. We paddled in increasingly high waves and finally after both Art's and Pete's canoes were shipping water, we turned back to the old campsite. Wind-bound for another rotten day. Had dinner and then left our camp once more with a dying wind. Paddled about 8 miles in the evening, making land about 11 PM on a very rough, windy, stony shore. Again the other two canoes were swamped in the landing and we were forced to dry our supplies for the second time this day. Bugs made a fierce chorus of welcome, but seemed strangely satisfied with hovering in a cloud around our heads, disconcerting, but painless.

Peter | JULY 2, 1955, BLACK LAKE

Everyone was very anxious to get away today. We got up early and loaded the canoes thinking to make it to the near side of the portage by evening. Once we got out on the water, we were loaded so heavily that the small waves broke over the sides and we had to turn back. With a normally

Tyrrell

The Hudson's Bay Company's trading post of Fond du Lac, near the east end of the lake (Athabasca) was found to be deserted, and we continued eastward over our track of last year until we reached the north shore of Black Lake, where the Indian canoe route strikes off to the north. Here we were to leave all beaten paths, and to strike into the unknown wilderness, without any other guide than the little Indian map obtained the year before.

loaded canoe, it would be no trick to go out on to the lake today, but with our load we took in too much water. Skip's canoe was okay, but Art's and mine had about an inch of water in the bottom. Some of the food got wet and we had to spread it out to dry. We sat around camp waiting for the wind and waves to go down. Finally at about seven, the waves were low enough to risk, and we started out again. After we traveled the first mile in pretty rough water, we got in the shelter of a large long island and had smooth going. We camped at a little point about half way. When we landed, we were out of the shelter of the island and the waves were big again. We landed on a rock beach and once the bows hit, the big waves starting crashing in over the stern. Skip got his stuff out all right, but we got water in and soaked a little oatmeal, while Art almost swamped. We spread the wet food out on a big rock shelf to dry and built a fire. The mosquitoes were so thick here that one's back was completely covered with them; looked like fur; could hardly see the shirt.

Skip | JULY 3, BLACK LAKE

Woke again to the steady hum of insects, but prepared breakfast with comparative ease. The wind of the night before died to a sticky, low-ceilinged calm and we left camp with certain misgivings about the weather. But by noon the clouds had disappeared and blue sky and sunshine combined to make a "shirts off" afternoon. Arrived at Wolverine (Black Lake) portage about 1 PM and after a brief lunch, we made one trip across the 2 ½-mile portage. Swamps, hills and our inactivity of the last week or so made this a bitch of a portage. Once again, soggy feet, sticky, sweaty body, bitten hands and neck, buzzing face and aching shoulders; the frustration of a long summer portage. But, a swim and light walk back forgets all. Camped on the Black Lake side of the portage, hoping to complete the carry tomorrow.

Peter | JULY 3, BLACK LAKE

The mosquito netting on the tent was black with mosquitoes this morning. My day to wash dishes too! The water was dead calm and the sky looked ominous, so we ate and got going in a hurry. It was an easy trip out. We found the entrance to the portage without much trouble and got everything on shore. We decided to take the boxes and canoes over first, as we could leave them at the other side safe from animals. I tied my paddles in and also tried rigging up a tump between them to take some of the weight off of my shoulder. It turned out to be a big help. George took a box on a tumpline and went across with me. We two were the first. I got about a third of the way across, then we came to a big, deep swamp. After hunting around for a time, we found the route straight across the deep part. I took off with the canoe and dragged it through to dry land on the other side. George had no trouble with his box, but Bruce and Joe carrying similar ones had to stop often and were in a bad way. George was a big help to me and we actually had a good time. The portage really brought us together like nothing else would. About three-quarters of a mile further, we came to another deep swamp and I went on in up to my crotch. After this was passed, we started climbing up and down until finally, we got to the lake. Skip was right behind and we started back together, meeting Art, Bruce and Joe on the way. When we got back, we decided to wait for Art before taking another load across. We went on the shore for a ways and went for a swim. All during the day the black flies, horse flies and mosquitoes had been very bad. Now on this side, they were even worse.

When Art got back, we decided to camp on this side and make the next three trips the next day. I was tired, but not exhausted. We had a roast beef and all the trimmings. It looked like a good night, so Art didn't bother to cover all of the packs with the tarp and I didn't put the extra cover over our tent.

Skip | JULY 4, BLACK LAKE

July 4th greeted us with a dreary rain squall. Breakfast was a very damp affair and I'm lying in the tent now hoping for clearing weather. By lunch the skies were clear, so after the usual pause of hardtack etc., we carried our second load across the portage. The second time through it was much easier: sunshine, easy load and a good rest. My back is very sore but doesn't seem to be getting any worse. It recuperates quickly after each strain . . . here's hoping it holds out. I'm slowly getting mentally adjusted to the mosquitoes.

They are much worse than I have ever experienced before, but certainly not unbearable, especially if one doesn't panic; most of them don't bite, they just buzz around.

Skip | JULY 5, CHIPMAN PORTAGE

Completed this 2½-mile monster. Three trips totaling approx. 12 miles pretty well finished me. Draft boards, Dana, Hanover, geology, skiing, cruising the Caribbean, mesh in the plodding rhythm of a well-loaded trail and generally drown out the thoughts of "why the hell am I here?"; "never again!" And then when it is over, even the most forbidding bush becomes a warm, friendly camp; and pride, satisfaction, mingle comfortably with fatigue and the luxury of a warm sleeping bag.

Peter | JULY 5, CHIPMAN PORTAGE

We finished Chipman portage today. George and I carried over our last two loads by noon. The day before, I carried a heavy load on a tump alone. I liked it and I am not sore today. Skip, George and I had one last swim at the old spot at the beginning of the portage and then George and I carried over our last loads and explored the small lake at the end of the portage. It is about a mile long and we found the next portage leading out of the far end, also about a mile. We came back and set up camp at the end of the Chipman portage and crawled into the tent to wait for the rest. George and I were on pretty good terms by now and we talked about our experiences in prep school and at Harvard and everyone showed up and we cooked dinner. I think Art is getting a raw deal in having Joe as bow man. He is sure lazy. All he does is eat a lot and avoid all the work he possibly can.

The smoke from forest fires was very thick tonight. Art thinks there is some danger.

Skip | JULY 6, NO NAME LAKES

Continued our "walking ways" today, completing 3 small portages; then coming to a rather inglorious end at a small "drag-over" into a well-used campsite on a small hill during a very cold rain shower. It has been 3 days now since we have paddled to any extent and the sore shoulders of lake travel have been forgotten. The tiny lakes which dot this stony, rugged country remind me of the quiet, isolated ponds of Dreiser's stories; rocky, wooded shores, many small islands, dark mysterious waters perched in small pockets between the rising ridges.

Peter | JULY 6, NO NAME LAKES

I slept very hard last night for about ten hours and still feel groggy this morning. George and I got our canoe loaded early and headed across the lake to the next portage before the rest. This portage is about a mile long and dry all the way. I made five trips. George made six, helping out Art who was slowed down by his heavy camera box and by Joe, who shirked again. We got all through by about five, loaded up the canoe and went on through the next lake for about 2 mi. until we came to a short portage of about one hundred yards. We got everything across and camped on top of a hill on the far side. It started to rain as we began the portage, stopped when we finished and got everything under cover. It has been remarkably dry so far this summer.

Skip | JULY 7, CHIPMAN LAKE

Today we finished the first series of "height-of-land" portages and arrived at the southern end of this moderate size lake (about 5 miles long). We started off with jackets in a very cool morning, huddled forms shuffling about. The entire day was a cool, bright, windy, bugless ideal of the "friendly Arctic." The portages were short and dry; the lakes again that curious beauty of mystery . . . all creating a sense of the first and perhaps most strenuous part of the trip completed and the first test of our party's worth. This bay of the lake is a beautiful E-W body of water surrounded by wooded, rolling shores. We are sitting around a swirling campfire and a pot of tea.

Peter | JULY 7, CHIPMAN LAKE

When we got up and had breakfast about 8:30, it was pretty cold compared to the weather we had been having; too cold for me in a wool shirt.

It still takes us a long time to get underway after breakfast. We didn't leave until 10:30. We went through a fairly long lake, through rough wind and water to the next portage twenty-three chains long. By the time we got over this we had lunch on the far side. Art took some movies of us bringing up our last loads and then shot a scene of us eating lunch and loading the canoes. It was still pretty cold after lunch. We paddled a short distance to the next portage, only two chains long, leading into a little "pot-hole" of a lake, hardly a quarter of a mile across. We saved hardly any distance by going through all the trouble of loading and unloading. The next portage was seven chains to an equally small lake out of which the last portage, twenty-one chains, led to Chipman Lake. George and I decided to skip the lake entirely and follow a trail that led around it and that connected with the last portage trail. I think we saved a lot of time and trouble and we finished way before the others, who paddled across the small lake. I was pretty tired after walking all that way, but there was nothing else to do, so I went back and helped the others get across the last portage. Joe shirked again. He only made two trips, besides which he won't do any of the work around camp.

We camped beside Chipman Lake on a high rocky cliff, windblown and free of mosquitoes. Art broke out one of the cans of ham and we feasted. Then everyone sat around drinking tea until midnight. The night was so cold I got out my parka over the wool shirt. If it is this cold this early in the trip, I hope it won't get too cold later on.

We won't get through before the middle of September and I only have in reserve now, one light sweater and a down vest.

Skip | JULY 8, CHIPMAN LAKE

After 5 days of walking and carrying with incidental puddle-hopping in the canoe, we took a very welcome day off here at the southern end of Chipman Lake. Odd jobs and washing took care of the morning; in the afternoon I tried some deep-water fishing. It seems that trolling just isn't my game . . . Algoma and Quebec also yielded nothing to the deeply sunk spoon. After dinner we found a cave in the surrounding rocks and spent the early evening photographing chunks of ice from the cave with the very beautiful surrounding country in the background.

Bed about 11 PM; temp 34F in the tent. It has been very cold today with grey, wintry clouds continually overhead . . . preview of things to come?

Peter | JULY 8, CHIPMAN LAKE

A good day; warm and sunny with a few clouds. We decided to have a day of rest today. Everyone got up late and sat around until lunch. I

Quiet water on the Chipman River, approaching Bompas Lake. Courtesy Creigh Moffatt.

got a little fed up and went for a walk before lunch and got back after it was over. George had been out in the morning with his .22 looking for grouse, but hadn't seen any. While I was washing dishes, Art scared one up right in camp and George was off again for the afternoon. I took a long walk around the shore to see if I could find any grouse, but I didn't see a one. I had a violent desire for guns and a chance to use them; all kinds, pistols, .22's, high-powered rifles, just to carry them around and shoot. I guess I have never grown out of my childhood passion for guns. I would like most of all to go on a long trip in game country with a rifle alone or with one other person and live off the land.

The spruce woods were very open with hardly any underbrush and a deep carpet of moss. It will be interesting to see how the woods change as we go further north. Two pounds of macaroni in the glop and it all disappeared in short order. A new record so far! Probably because it was pretty cool all day today; thirty-four degrees F. at 11:30 when we went to bed.

Skip | JULY 9, CHIPMAN LAKE

Paddled the entire length of Chipman Lake today and continued upstream on the Chipman River as far as the first portage. The day was just perfect for lake travel; faint cooling north breeze, blue sunny sky with dancing white clouds above; shirts off for the first time in a week. We are now camped at the first small rapid of the river on a flat, open, bugless point. The trees seem to have been cleared from the point, providing an open view of white water and circling back eddies; very pleasant as the smell of boiling glop pervades the hungry dreams of 6 tired, "not so iron men."

Skip | JULY 10, BOMPAS LAKE

Completed 3 more portages around small rapids, longest about ½ mile, today and entered Bompas Lake. We traveled all day under the hazy gloom of a smoke-filled sky. Fires to the south send smoke, ashes and heavy acrid air. The packs and still water are covered with white ash and our eyes smart and run continually. The sun appears as a dull, red-orange ball and at times resembles surrealistic pictures of science-fiction planets. As we paddled late in the evening on Bompas Lake, the breeze died and with it the airborne smoke slowly settled on the lake and the surrounding hills and valleys like a morning mist. The entire scene was an eerie, quiet, loon-interrupted resemblance of the Scottish moors . . . all we would have needed to complete the illusion was a medieval castle perched, half-hidden amid the spruce.

In the evening after dinner, Bruce came back to camp with a 7-lb. lake trout which I cleaned for a morning supplement to the usual oats and coffee.

Skip | JULY 11, BOMPAS LAKE

Photography dominated this day's activities. Taking the lake trout supplement as the keynote for an outstanding breakfast, Art and I made a detailed sequence of breakfast preparations. This involved a few film feet of each action from different camera angles. The entire process took about 2 hrs. The pattern of our movie taking is a distant shot of the general subject followed by a close-up of the detailed action. Each of these shifts must also be accompanied by a shift in angle so that the break in the scenes will not be sudden and distracting.

Leisurely swim, washing and breaking camp followed, and noon found us setting ponchos for a swift sail to the NE corner of the lake; en route, we stopped at a small, rocky island with a tern's nest; spent about 2 hrs. photographing the remarkable display of parental concern of the two adults and the shivering obedience of the fluffball offspring. Continued on to the portage into Selwyn Lake; couldn't find it right away and as the light was fading we set camp on a rocky point for the night.

Peter | JULY 11, BOMPAS LAKE

A lazy day! Skip fried the fish for breakfast and Art got movies of the process. We all ate so much that everyone laid around for an hour or two.

It was past noon when we shoved off into a strong south wind that was pushing us down the lake in the direction that we wanted to go. We were

Easy miles on Bompas Lake. Courtesy Creigh Moffatt.

drifting along when we came by a close bare little rock island. A couple of terns resting there came swooping out and tried to fight us off. They are a beautiful bird like a large white swallow. These turned out to be Arctic terns, and Art got some good movies of them actually landing on our heads and pecking at us in an effort to scare us off. We spent nearly two hours there and then shoved off and had lunch.

After we got down to the north end of the lake, we looked around for the portage, but couldn't find it. We paddled up two rapids, but couldn't go any further so we turned back and found a good campsite on the lake. Before dinner, I took George's .22 and walked around in the bush to see if I could find a spruce hen. Sure enough, I flushed one. She wouldn't give me a very good shot, but she finally landed in a tree, so I took a long shot and got her in the neck. After dinner, George and I fried the meat. There was enough to make a small meal for one man, and it turned out to be surprisingly good; tender if not cooked too much.

I am getting tired of these people though and feel estranged from the whole group. An outsider, I don't like the way they do things and George and I don't mix. I think I would much rather be taking the trip alone or with one other person. With this group, it is too much like an excursion of a bunch of jolly good fellows out for a good time. I would like to see much more of the country and have it come close. It would be a big factor in my life, my personality.

Skip | JULY 12, SELWYN LAKE

We have now completed about 12 portages and have entered the southern waters of Selwyn Lake. This very large lake (nearly 45 miles long) marks the northern limits of winter trap lines of the Indians. North of these shores, the country is left to caribou, barrens, perhaps some roaming hunters, and an occasional bunch of canoeing newcomers.

Already the maps are far from realistic. Uncharted islands appear quite often and channels become necks of land; lakes have unknown openings; rapids and portages appear almost anywhere.

Beautiful morning spent with more movie sequences; tern island, caribou horns . . .

Two small portages into a pot hole and then ½-mile portage into the big lake. Hot as hell with flies and bull dogs galore. Seems as if a hatch of black flies has appeared in my hair; beard itches; back seems to be getting a little worse since this string of portages. Coming few days of lake travel should help out; very tired.

Peter | JULY 12, SELWYN LAKE

More time wasted! We sit up late at night and then get up early because the sun heats up the tents. After breakfast everyone sort of dozes around 'til 11:00 or noon. Art wanted to take pictures of us landing on a rock island so he would have something leading up to the tern shots. Then we spent a long time looking for the portage. We got our stuff across a narrow neck of land into a small pond, but we couldn't find the trail from there.

George is getting to be a real bastard in my book; throws the packs

Peter Franck using his paddles as a portage yoke. Courtesy Creigh Moffatt.

around and doesn't do what I tell him as a stern man. The way I feel now, I intend to cut myself off from the others as much as possible and spend more time on the country. I shall have dealings with the others just as necessary to get along.

Art just got back from exploring and bushwhacking, trying to find the portage trail. We found that we were fourteen chains from a pot-hole out of which the portage to Selwyn Lake led. We made this alright and paddled a few miles on Selwyn, making camp on a rocky point.

Selwyn Lake looks like a long, narrow finger of water forking up the middle. It is 50 mi. long and seems just like a broad, calm river.

Skip | JULY 13, SELWYN LAKE

Best weather to date; paddled nude most of the day. We traveled all day on this long lake, totaled 20 miles; best run to date. The perfection of the day was only marred by pestering, sea-faring bulldog flies, which leads me to speculate that part of the charm and appeal of this life lies in the curious mixture of the ideal and the bothersome. Perhaps the flies, and sudden rains, and laboring head winds and sore muscles are precious in that they intensify the simple beauty and genuine value of a perfect day.

Peter | JULY 13, SELWYN LAKE

Dawned bright and clear with little wind from the south. My boots are starting to go. The leather is okay, but on the left foot, the new sole I had put on is starting to come off. I tried to fix it with Joe's stitcher, but without much success. Finally I got some wood screws out of the repair kit and fastened them pretty tightly.

We made about 20 mi. today, passing the fork in Selwyn Lake and sticking pretty close to the left shore. When we made camp, the smoke closed in and cinders were falling all around. Wherever we go, we seem to be followed by these fires.

I have given up trying to hold my temperament to any one level or aim. One day I am in one mood and the next, I am an entirely different person.

Skip | JULY 14, SELWYN LAKE

Entered the NW Territories today and paddled continuously until 9 PM, covering the great northern bay of this lake; finally stopping on a rocky, open point; beautifully muted with lichens and moss. If this is a preview of the Barrens, they'll be most welcome. No flies to speak of, and even without the security of enclosing trees and bush, the airy freedom of open country is refreshing and delightful. The duality of leadership for this adventure which heretofore had existed only in the minds of the other guys and in such chores of experience as setting camp and cooking, was given a good boost in my mind today, when the various alternatives and decisions of navigating this difficult region of water-land became a matter of two heads rather than one. At times, Art seems genuinely dependent upon some sort of consultation and recognizes the value of my opinion and judgments in certain areas; makes me feel really good.

Peter | JULY 14, SELWYN LAKE

Clear again. We all have ravenous appetites and are still hungry after even the largest meal. I am thinking very seriously now of watching and marking down the way and going on this trip again some time with one other person. I know Rich Gordon would like to go on such a trip, but whether he could or not would be another problem.

Canoeing was very tiring today. The wind blew from the side and tended to swing the stern so that I had to keep drawing the paddle toward me. Still, we kept paddling until 6:00 when Art asked us to try for some islands at the mouth of the bay in which the portage lies. Fortunately, the lake had calmed to dead still by this time and we made it to a beautiful open camp on a small island by 9:00. There was still plenty of daylight so we had no trouble making camp. George lazed along all day, letting his paddle just float through the water most of the time and reading a book, open and lying in the bottom of the canoe. I had to take about three strokes to his two to keep up with the rest. I don't know what to make of him. He seems perfectly agreeable and even conscientious in camp, but get him in a canoe and he sloughs off.

Skip | JULY 15, SELWYN LAKE

Spent the day in camp and enjoyed the idleness of reading, loafing, unsuccessful fishing, canoe patching and very peaceful dozing outside. A certain luxurious oneness seems to engulf me when I lie down on the moss in warmth and breeziness . . . to feel my whole body against the earth and my nose close to the smells of life and growth. At times the hope, desire and need of a life with at least some of the sky and woods, and fields, and water is incredibly urgent.

It is almost a month now since leaving home and over 2 weeks since leaving Stony Rapids and the convenience of the HBC store, and already the lack of food, or perhaps the psychological need for a little extra left in the pot is beginning to affect the party. George and Joe started the open recognition of selfishness as a joke on themselves. Obvious gluttony and scheming became an irreverent virtue. This soon infected the rest of the gang, and now as the joke begins to wear off, the rush for an extra portion becomes tense. I hope the inevitable crisis comes soon, is effectively dealt with and not too painful for anyone. George is an example of an intelligent guy who perverts the recognition of man's essential selfishness and egotism to serve as an excuse and justification for those attitudes, sometimes to the extent that any consideration and even the slightest altruism falls as hypocrisy.

Wind changing to the N., cold.

TRANSITION

TYRRELL, 1893	LOCATION	MOFFATT, 1955
July 20	Wholdaia Lake (height-of-land)	July 17–25
TOTAL: 14 days		TOTAL: 23 days
July 22–26	Hinde Lake	July 28
July 27	Boyd Lake	August 1–3

Skip | JULY 16, SELWYN LAKE

Arrived at the southern end of this "height-of-land" portage today after a short paddle of about 8 miles and a 3-hr picture-taking session . . . sequences of examining Indian graves and finding artifacts.

When we got to the portage it was close to 6 PM and after unloading the canoes and carrying our supplies about 300 yds. along the portage, I decided to walk over to the other lake. We had not done much walking for a few days and as I started out my legs felt rather rubbery. Trip over was uneventful, over a good, dry, generally downhill trail. Wholdaia Lake has high rock cliffs on its E shore; low wooded hills to the W; many islands. The sky is filled with smoke. On my return to camp, my legs gave out frequently. I felt woozy and aching, head spinning. Wonder what that is all about? The usual meal of glop fixed things up pretty well, but the prospect of future, possibly more intense, physical problems is not pleasant.

Tyrrell

While within the forest we had been tormented both day and night by immense swarms of mosquitos, but now in the more open country, the black flies made it almost impossible to move about with any portions of our hands or faces uncovered.

Bruce LeFavour with a pink quartzite arrow head, northern shore of Selwyn Lake just south of the height-of-land. Courtesy Creigh Moffatt.

Wildfire smoke along the northeastern shore of Wholdaia Lake. Courtesy Creigh Moffatt.

Skip | JULY 17, WHOLDAIA LAKE

We started out this morning traveling in smoke-free air for the first time in many days. At last we thought we were beyond the fire line. And then as we approached the portage, more fires appeared very close to the portage itself and we again entered the acrid gloom of burning country. Art characterized our feelings pretty well when he ended the day with, "Ain't it the shits!"

Started the portage about 10:30 AM and finally completed the 1½-mi jaunt around 9 PM. Most of the day was spent photographing the nearby forest fire. Four of us took a canoe and paddled ½ mi across a bay to the very foot of the fire. We hiked along a series of eskers on the edge of the fire and were right on the spot as the spruce and birch rose in flames like gigantic ceremonial torches. As we watched, the fire seemed to take on almost anthropomorphic characteristics; its movements seemed to follow a battle plan as it crept along the forest floor, extending its flanks and then engulfing the isolated tree as the enemy in a rush of sound and flame.

Skip | JULY 18, WHOLDAIA LAKE

This morning the fires were pretty well subdued. Small, smoldering areas could be distinguished through the drifting smoke and nude, charred, standing trunks. After breakfast, Art and I set out some rotten bully beef and decoyed Canada Jays for the movies. The birds were quite tame, grabbing the meat within a few feet of us. Good sequence to work into breakfast shots.

Stopped for lunch during a rain squall . . . cold, windy, short-lived, clearing in the afternoon. Paddled until the N wind freshened and forced us ashore in the lea of a swampy island . . . camp is on a small rise midst muskeg and stunted spruce; flies are bad. Poplar has died out since Selwyn and the spruce are scrawny.

As we sit around the fire this evening, the entire southern sky is black and rumbling, foretelling coming storm; tents double secure; canoes well sheltered.

Peter | JULY 18, WHOLDAIA LAKE

The Canada Jays were thick around the meat that we had thrown away, so Art got some great pictures of these. We didn't get started until about noon. I made a deal with Joe, giving him four packs of cigarettes for the privilege of using his maps as I go along in the canoe, so now I can follow our route as we move and get used to orienting the country with the map. Even if I never make this trip again, this will be good practice.

Using these 8 mi. to the inch maps, all the small islands and all but the largest features in the landscape are eliminated, but some small, medium-sized islands are left out while others the same size are included, seemingly at random. This is the most confusing part of the maps.

Today, we have been seeing tundra for the first time; broad fields of moss going down to the water's edge. No trees on them. They are frozen under the first foot or so of moss. They occur here and there, widely separated now. Tyrrell mentions them in his journals and says that they stop at tree line where the sphagnum moss cannot grow for lack of shade.

We had made about 4 mi. when it started to rain. George and I covered the load and we pulled up to eat lunch. There was some debate as to whether or not we should camp, but the only place was on top of one of those bogs, so we sat in the canoes and pretty soon the rain stopped. George looked on top of the tundra and said it was wet, no firewood, so on we went.

The sun finally came out for a brief space, but went back in again. It was calm for a while in the afternoon and Art seemed determined to go on to the near side of the portage over a little neck of land that would save us two days' paddle, but the wind came up strong dead against us . . . It looked like rain and we were all shipping water, so we decided to camp on a little hill. It was not a bad spot and we battened everything down to prepare for the rain. It started to come after dinner, but didn't really start until we went to bed. There were several violent thunderstorms all night and the tent was almost blown away. The rain came in almost a solid torrent. I lay awake and thought about what a savage display of power this was, yet it is as if the country let its guard down for an instant and showed its hard, dangerous side.

Skip | JULY 19, WHOLDAIA LAKE

Experienced one of the most terrifying thunderstorms of my life last night. All night the sky was lighted with startling flashes of lightning, closely followed by shaking crashes of thunder. The rain merged into a steady sheet of water, disguising any individual raindrops in the pulsing roar of a north wind. Tents seemed ready to be torn from their stakes at any moment.

Breakfast was a rather soggy chore, helped somewhat by semi-dry wood found beneath a spruce fall, and by gradually clearing skies; winds are finally easing.

Left camp in a sticky, calm gloom of another threatening storm and paddled to a swampy bog where we found the short portage across a neck of land leading into the northern portion of Wholdaia Lake. We are camped on a beautiful lichen-covered rocky rise on the western shore of a small island. Sunset and calm create a mirrored spectacle of northern pastel splendor.

Skip | JULY 20, WHOLDAIA LAKE

The beauty of last evening continued today; clear morning, sparkling and warm. As we pushed off from this gem of a camp, after taking two short film sequences, we continued westward with the sun on our stern; hot, with a slight breeze, and then as we turned northeast, the wind shifted easterly and freshened. Clouds threatened rain but none fell. We spent a few hours examining one of the numerous peat bogs along these shores. The brown peat is overlain by small green cover and low bushes. About a foot beneath the surface permanent ice is imbedded in hard packed peat. The entire bog resembles a glacier in its layered structure and probably moves in a similar manner down the surface of a slope.

Camped on a very small, exposed island with rain threatening.

Peter | JULY 20, WHOLDAIA LAKE

A clear, calm, beautiful day. For once, everyone mobilized right after breakfast. Only George was nowhere to be found. After I took down the tent and got everything packed away, I had a good wash and even washed my blue jeans. Then George showed up and we got the canoe in the water. I paddled all morning with no shirt and got a sunburn. It was still clear at lunch. Later, long, wispy clouds began to trail across the sky and black clouds were approaching.

About 3:30, we stopped at a tundra with a very steep bank and a sandy beach. When we got on top, we found that it was very open and relatively dry, dry enough to sit on. I got some pictures of everyone walking around here and digging through the moss; finding ice which we found everywhere at a depth of about one foot. The moss was springy and soft and covered with lichens. The whole place was delightful. It was wind-blown enough so that there were no black flies or mosquitoes. In fact, flies have been very scarce for the last two weeks. Evenings around the campfire have been relatively untroubled until quite late.

The sand beach in front of this little tundra is beautiful, fine-grained with a very gradual slope. Everyone, including Art, went for a swim here. On our way to this tundra, the wind was strong against us, from the north, while the clouds came up from the south, as they usually do. Still bucking this headwind, we made it 6 mi. further to a small, bare hill on the point in the narrow channel between the large island and the shore. The clouds haven't gotten any worse, but there is a constant muttering of thunder and a new bank of clouds that look like rain coming from the east. Art thought he heard sandhill cranes here.

Skip | JULY 21, WHOLDAIA LAKE

The rain of last night stopped by the time I crawled out of the tent to begin breakfast, but the gloom and oppressive overcast continued throughout the day. After bucking a considerable headwind all afternoon, we were forced ashore on an open tundra plain by the return of the rain. These patches of open tundra are intermittent reminders of the rapidly changing vegetation. Ever since Selwyn Lake, the poplar/birch trees were dying out until now even the scrawniest specimen is cause for comment. Scraggly spruce trees growing in fringes and clusters are the main tree cover now. Numerous ridges of lichen-covered, rounded bedrock can be seen separated at intervals by low, open plains underlain by peat bogs, some of which resemble huge football fields completely bare of trees and forming a small cliff at the shoreline.

The important problem of when and where to camp is creating somewhat of an issue for our party, and the serious threat of disunity and grumbling seems to be primarily caused by Art's method of handling such affairs. Two alternatives seem open to him. Either assume complete leadership, making all decisions; or submit to the will of the group. Art's tendency is to try and make each move a group decision and still maintain leadership. This leads to asking opinions, then trying to sway differing views and finally following his own opinion anyway; usually the cause for some grumbling no matter what the outcome.

Peter | JULY 21, WHOLDAIA LAKE

The wind almost blew our tent down last night, far too rough to travel. We are holed up here for the day. I took a walk inland down the point about 2 mi. and came upon a big tundra where the point joins the mainland and a high hill behind this tundra. I got an eerie feeling of loneliness and smallness crossing this with the wind blowing hard. I climbed a hill and got a splendid view of the surrounding country. The tundra is becoming more and more extensive behind the fringe of trees along the water.

Directly to the east, I could see a large, rocky mountain far away. For some reason, it fascinated me and I would sure like to climb it some day.

I got back in time for lunch and spent the afternoon hunting for spruce grouse without success. I flushed one male, but it got out of there so fast that I couldn't get a shot. I think the hens with broods are the only ones that offer easy targets.

The sky is still overcast with high clouds and the wind still strong.

Skip | JULY 22, WHOLDAIA LAKE

Wind-bound on Wholdaia! The force and frequency of these storms, combined with the rolling tundra and the scrubby spruce, emphasizes that we are finally, truly in the North country.

Art is taking a shot of the interior of our tent while this is being written . . . Bruce reads Steinbeck on my left. Spent the morning photographing the storm-bound camp and the breaking seas; also developed a lead-in sequence for some of the bird shots (Art & binoculars). Spent the entire day here. The wind blew continually and although the overcast broke for the sun to shine for a few hours, as evening approaches, the sky is again heavy and dark, foreboding another windy night.

Made a detailed inventory of our food supply and we seem to be in good shape for about 50 more days. This brings us into the first part of September when we should likely reach the post at Baker Lake. Sugar and other sweets pose somewhat of a problem in as much as the longer we are away the more intense the sweet tooth becomes. However, minor rationing should take care of this.

While repacking my personal belongings this afternoon, I mused over the pictures of Dana and our Mt. Washington trip. An hour passed in memory with the dominant theme of hope that we can pick up somewhere after we left off so abruptly at the airport. I read through her letter and wonder about that question mark. All this contributes to the loneliness of my barrens.

The weather, the relative barrenness and the immobility of the day intensify the loneliness of this country. The isolation of man in time, and in nature is unmistakable here. Picture of a young man sitting in the lee of a big rock on the barren shore of a white-capped, grey-tossed expanse, reading Shaw (*Man & Superman*).

Skip | JULY 23, WHOLDAIA LAKE

Woke up this morning to a strong southerly wind, making it impossible to travel again today. The wind, however, was warm and occasional breaks in the overcast made a pleasant day for wind-bound projects. After breakfast, Art and I packed a lunch and the cameras for a day of hiking and filming. Birds were our primary objective. We concentrated on a high, open ridge about five miles from camp and got some good close-ups of Yellowlegs and Harris Sparrow; also some shots of the tundra. Had lunch in brilliant, windy sunshine and then continued with the camera. About 5 PM a large dark cloud bank appeared in the north and within

20 minutes the temperature had dropped at least 20 degrees and a hard, driving rain replaced the lazy sunshine. The walk back to camp was cold and wet. We arrived soaked to the skin and decided to cook dinner right away. Cold, wet and the pot refusing to boil! At last the tell-tale bubbles and a hot meal of glop, pudding and tea. Pete had not returned from his hike by the time dinner was over and I hope he will turn up before dark; certainly don't envy the poor guy. Am now dry and relatively warm in the tent with pajamas and wool socks. Rain seems to be easing.

The unpleasantness of this late afternoon, although brief, makes me think of what it will be like during 3 or 4 days of continual rain. Grim times may be ahead.

Peter | JULY 23, WHOLDAIA LAKE

The wind is far too strong to paddle today; still cloudy. It looks somewhat like rain. Last night and this morning are warm, sixty degrees. After breakfast, we all went our ways; George to hunt grouse, Art and Skip trying to take pictures of birds, and I to take a long walk.

I took my lunch and set out climbing the first hill that I had climbed the day before. I headed from there directly south-southeast to another bare hill about 1.5 mi. from the first. From this hill, I could see that large rocky mountain to the east very clearly and it really fascinated me. So, against my better judgment, I started toward it, cutting down to Lone Lake and following along its shore. The country changes a lot. Here it happens to be high, so there is dry ground with tall trees and little undergrowth, but a little further on, you go down into a hollow and are walking in swamp, plowing through a thick tangle of stunted spruce.

I followed Lone Lake until I got to an esker going off to the east. I found a fine Indian campsite there, where the esker joined the lake, but found no arrow heads. I didn't look thoroughly though. I found the esker excellent walking and quite striking in appearance. It is a mound of sand like a mole tunnel, running along fairly straight. On top, it is open and sandy, while there is swamp and lakes on both sides. I walked on this esker for 3 mi. and then went around a big lake and climbed a bare hill. From there, I could see the rock mountain and it didn't look a bit bigger than it had from the hill near camp. At this point the sky cleared and bright sun came out warm. The day was about half way through, so I decided to turn back. I had lunch on the esker.

I was a little scared I wouldn't be able to find my way back and was feeling pretty lonely by this time. This country really makes a person feel small and lost, wandering in a great immensity, much more so than the mountains. I went back to Lone Lake along the esker and walked down along it until I felt it was time to turn off to get to the second high, bare hill from which I could see the first one near camp. At this time the sun went under a solid bank of black clouds. Walking in the trees, I couldn't see any of the landmarks. I came out on a big tundra, but could see nothing familiar and was heading in the wrong direction until I saw a sand bank way over on one side. I thought this looked familiar, so I walked over and took a look. Sure enough, there were my footprints from the morning. Without the sun, I had missed my orientation badly and continued to do so.

By this time it was getting late. I didn't know where I was and I was in the beginning of a panic. I came out on another big tundra that looked totally unfamiliar, but I walked all the way across it and saw that it was the one facing the second hill. I could see the first hill and started toward it. At this point it started to rain. I got stuck in some pretty deep swamps and thought I was lost again, but I finally came out on the first hill. Here I thought my troubles were over, but they were just beginning. I came out too far down the shore and headed in the wrong direction; really panicked by this time. I finally retraced my steps and came out on the tundra again, but I still had a few bad moments before I got back to camp, thoroughly soaked. I had been walking for ten hours. The others had given me up for lost and were going to look for me tomorrow. Art and I sat up drying clothes for a long time after the others had gone to bed. He plans to spend a month in the Sierra making a family movie the summer after next. It was wonderful to be back at camp and to be able to talk to somebody after wandering in this desolate country, lost for half the time.

Skip | JULY 24, WHOLDAIA LAKE

Climbed into wet socks and Levis this morning at 6 AM and found a pastel green sky with dark, windblown clouds and 40F. Wind made it very cold and rain of the night before made the cook fire a problem, but finally got things going and got the gang up about 8:15. Peter had returned to camp early last night and seems fine; perhaps a little hungrier than other mornings.

Long underwear and wool hat are the order of the day. Yellow slicker has been the outer layer for past 3 days. With the wind again heading us, but easing, we hope to be off this afternoon for a cold, tough paddle to the mouth of the Dubawnt R.

PM: instead of continuing to lessen, the wind shifted to the W and freshened at noon and so for the third day in a row, the waves and penetrating cold of the wind bound us to our Wholdaia camp. With annoying regularity, each passing cloud dumps a small shower of rain in its shadow and makes the cold even more noticeable. Campfire blazed all day and much of the chatter concerned the prospects of a similar day on the windswept, woodless barrens. Dubawnt Lake looms in the distance, with anticipation and apprehension, we wonder, will it be ice-bound? And, if so, how will we manage?

Skip | JULY 25, WHOLDAIA LAKE

Another day of wind, dulling cold and pounding waves. We all are hoping that stories of "five day blows" will live up to expectations and end the foul weather tomorrow. The realization that prolonged periods of immobility eat into our supplies with no increase in mileage to balance the scale creeps into the minds of everyone. The leaden sky seems to form an infinite lid over us, enclosing the wind and cold in this huge pot of tossing water, permitting only occasional glimpses of blue sky and sunshine. With the necessity of traveling about 600 miles before reaching Baker Lake and new supplies, our party has adopted a versatile schedule primarily dependent on the weather. Whenever it is possible to travel, we will move, day or night, and will set our sleep accordingly. The twilight makes night travel possible and approaching winter seems to insist upon movement.

10 PM. True to my previous words, just after I had crawled into my sleeping bag for what seemed to be another windy night, Art called to me that the wind was easing and to come out and take a look. Within 45

minutes camp was struck, the canoes loaded and the six of us paid our own personal farewells to this Wholdaia prison. We paddled until 1:30 AM, when the increased overcast cancelled out the arctic twilight and it became impossible to read the map or the shoreline. We pulled into what appeared to be a beach through the darkness, erected a canvas shelter against the wind, built a large fire and waited with numerous cups of tea for dawn.

Peter | JULY 25, WHOLDAIA LAKE

Overcast and very windy, so we are stuck here a fourth day. It is beginning to get on my nerves. I read Thomas Wolfe and did a little hunting. It is cold again, about forty-five degrees. All I have in reserve now is one light sweater. This down vest is not as good as I expected it to be. I hope it never gets much colder than this. After dinner the waves began to calm down and around 10:00 Art suddenly decided to move out. It was cold and a little windy but everyone was so glad to get out that no one minded.

It was quite dark but we managed to find our way 7 mi. to where we thought the channel to the Dubawnt was. There we camped, leaving the stuff in the canoes and only boiling water to make tea.

Skip | JULY 26, DUBAWNT RIVER

About 4 AM the overcast lifted in the east and a beautiful red-orange dawn aroused us. We shot our first rapid of the trip shortly before leaving Wholdaia Lake and then, after a few small bays and a connecting outlet, we entered the Dubawnt, a wide, shallow, swift river at this head. We are camped at the first shallow rapid on the river and have enjoyed excellent fishing . . . 13 grayling within ½ hr.! After no real sleep for 36 hr., the prospect of a good meal and then the sack looms pleasantly.

Peter | JULY 26, DUBAWNT RIVER

We sat around drinking tea until 3:00 when it was light enough to travel. We found the narrows with no trouble and followed along until we came to the first big rapid. The river narrows down a lot and runs swift and deep for about seventy-five or one hundred yards. There was a large rock in the middle on the right side, leaving a narrow channel on the left. Out in the tail of the rapids, there are quite a few rocks just below the surface. Art ran it first and came through all right. Then I came down; I went all right until just before that big rock in the middle. I tried to turn in a little to get into the channel on the left, and when I did so, the current caught the stern and swung it around so that by the time that I got straightened out, I was too close to the left shore and the bow grazed against the large rock on the side. After this, I was so rattled that I couldn't see where I was going out in the tail, and so ran over a rounded boulder that was just awash. After that all went well and I pulled over to the side to empty the load and look at the canoe. There was a small dent in the bow where I had grazed against the shore, but the real damage was from the rock in the tail. The inner planking had a cracked place and the canvas was scraped. Fortunately, there was no real damage. If the rock had been sharp, it would have been a different story. Everyone is very nice about this and tells me to forget it, but George will use it as a weapon to disregard my commands and do as he damn well pleases, I feel sure. This certainly cannot happen again, or I will be a greater liability than an asset to everyone on the trip.

We went on from this rapid to the next lake, where we had breakfast. As soon as breakfast was over, we pushed on and made it to the first rapid in the Dubawnt by lunch. This was a very broad and shallow rapid and not deep enough to run in the canoes. We camped on the left bank, and I and Bruce got out fishing. The Arctic grayling were very abundant here and we had a tremendous meal. They must be scaled, but they make excellent eating. I went to bed early to make up for the night before.

Skip | JULY 27, DUBAWNT RIVER

The precious few hours of sunshine which we experienced yesterday gave way to heavy overcast this morning, finally turning into a steady drizzle about 4 PM. We made camp after lunch and a pot of "cold-weather" tea. The steady, gentle patter of rain on the tent reminds me of those lazy, annoying rains of the Albany country.

Although we only traveled about 2 hrs today, we made 8 miles or so and are now within an easy day travel of Hinde Lake. Each of the lakes to come seems spaced as a stepping-stone to one of the big challenges of the trip, Dubawnt Lake. We watch the lakes go by on the map with an eager eye, remembering Tyrrell's description of the ice-bound lake and discontinuous leads along the shorcline. Is that what we are approaching?

The end of firewood has not really touched us yet and we enjoy the fuel of the bush in the form of driftwood as well as the spacious vistas and distant horizons of the Barrens. From a distance, some of the hills and meadows resemble very well-kept fairways; clipped, rockless, and gently rolling in well-disciplined curves. On closer examination, the ground is composed of dried peat resembling stringy, compact sawdust and sandy soil imbedded with small stones. The damper portions are very similar to the muskeg farther south.

When the sun does shine, as it did last evening, the sunsets and evening hours are magnificent. The sun becomes a hub of shimmering light, centering in orange and then flowing outward into soft reds and yellows against the pastel blue-green background of the Arctic sky. Distances lose perspective in this shimmering vastness and the entire plains seem to be engulfed in an unrealistic bluish haze. But when it rains and blows, it's a bitch.

Peter | JULY 27, DUBAWNT RIVER

We made a short portage around the rapids and then went on downstream, getting into a long, fairly easy rapid that went down into a small lake.

The current was very swift, but the only danger was from big rocks just below the surface. I got through this all right and felt somewhat better about being in the stern.

There was a strong wind against us in the lake and black clouds were coming up fast behind. We made it into the outlet and went down stream through very easy rapids into a wide place in the river. Here we stopped to have lunch. Before we were finished, the rain came and we decided to stay put for the night. We put up the tarp and the rain set in slow and steady. It kept up most of the night.

Before we went to bed, we started talking about how we could avoid paying $200 extra for a private plane from Baker Lake to Churchill. Art suggested we might buy a thirty-foot whale boat from the Eskimo and sail it to Churchill or even on down to Moosanee. Skip went wild at this idea, as he loves to sail, and we talked and made plans for the next hour. Of course, it seems completely crazy from a practical point of view, but it was fun to talk about and would be a great adventure, as well as a good finish to the film. In any case, it looks like I am going to be a bit late for registration as the train from Churchill takes almost a week to get to Winnipeg.

Skip | JULY 28, HINDE LAKE

The day was dominated by beautiful, swirling, blowing, puffing, multicolored clouds which were continually changing position and texture against the background of light blue sky and the exciting tension of running a long succession of rapids. Three of the rapids required long consultation and finally, after much hemming and hawing and mentally diagramming various options, I led the way down. Art seems somewhat overly cautious, probably due to the risk of the camera equipment. On the second run, Bruce and I led again, and as we waited in the quiet pool below, Pete came down with word that Art had swamped. After considerable wait, the gray canoe appeared with two very bedraggled men paddling slowly toward us, one with a rather sheepish grin, the other with fear and relief mixing his features. A later check of supplies showed very little damage . . . ½ bag oatmeal, some wet hardtack and considerable quantities of dampened pride. The last rapid of the day was so exciting that the tension throughout the run and the release at the bottom were almost identical to those of a tight ski slalom run. A brief paddle below the rapids brought us to a campsite on a high esker overlooking Hinde Lake.

Skip | JULY 29, PTARMIGAN RAPID

We continued drying our wet supplies this morning, only to be soaked by another passing shower; but we are on the move again.

Tyrrell

The next morning, as we were . . . making for a high point with a huge boulder lying on its summit, one of the men drew my attention to an immense herd of caribou on the eastern shore. . . . The continuance of the exploration depended on our obtaining an abundant supply of meat, and the knowledge of this fact added to our excitement, as we stood in the midst of the tens of thousands of deer.

After checking our position against the remaining supplies and the approaching winter, we have adopted a new plan of action. Instead of eating around 9 AM and not leaving until nearly noon, I am now getting up at 7 AM, waking the rest who strike camp while I cook breakfast. Thus we are generally traveling by 9 AM; always barring rain or photography, or some other diversion.

Had a grumpy outbreak over the sugar situation. We are now ½ through the supply and only about ⅓ of the distance to Baker Lake. After much discussion, we decided to give each man a 5-day ration from each 5-lb bag, thus allowing about ⅙ lb/day. Each will carry his own supply and use it according to his taste. Hope it works.

Spent a good portion of the afternoon on a high, sandy esker on the NW shore of Hinde Lake. This area is abundant with eskers, timbered by huge white spruce, 40–50 ft. high, spaced evenly along a clear, gravelly floor. The esker generally extends along the shore for considerable distance until the water breaks through at some point, forming a large rapid. The view from these eskers is wonderful . . . the horizon is visible for 360 degrees and the alternating tundra, scattered lakes and spruce groves present a vast panorama of endless wilderness.

Skip | JULY 30, DUBAWNT RIVER

Doled out the sugar ration into six small cans. The four guys seem somewhat in love with the notion of individual rations which they can play with . . . great concern whether it should go over the oatmeal or into the tea. Not sure how Art feels about all this.

After portaging Ptarmigan Rapids, we continued traveling along the river through more eskers and moraines which seem to run on separate banks (moraines to the NE, eskers to the NW). Very disappointed we couldn't run the rapid; it definitely would have been a tricky challenge of waves and boulders, but well worth a try if the consequences of a mishap were not so great.

Along with the appearance of the characteristic eskers and large white spruce, this area around Hinde Lake and the river north to Boyd Lake show the return of hardwood trees (birch, some poplar) and considerable stands of mature black spruce. It is quite surprising that here within 20 miles of the extreme northern limit of the trees we would find such timber, while 40 miles to the south virtually none exist. The "country

Bruce LeFavour, left, and Art Moffatt on one of the numerous esker ridges, vicinity Hinde Lake. Courtesy Creigh Moffatt.

club" meadows also have disappeared in favor of wooded hills and large tracts of timber. Perhaps it is the appearance of the sandy soils of the esker and perhaps a rather anthropomorphic "last gasp" before the land is truly plunged into the treeless Barrens.

Days such as this certainly smack of the north; temp stayed in the 40s all day; grey, leaden skies hanging very low, giving a dull, steel-like coloring to everything and making the monochromatic rapids hard to analyze and difficult to run; our party perhaps best characterized by the gradually narrowing circle of men standing close to the campfire, holding steaming red bowls in both hands.

Peter | JULY 30, DUBAWNT RIVER

After looking at Ptarmigan Rapid, we decided it could be shot, but it would be easier and safer to portage. We portaged along the right shore, right from our camp. After we loaded and got started again, we ran two more fairly easy rapids without looking and stopped at a large sandy hill on the left bank. It was a very pleasant spot, ground cover of lichens and a few blueberries, as well as some evergreen that grows flat on the ground like a carpet. The esker was covered with huge white spruce with big trunks, very tall and straight. The hill was quite high and steep, and from it you could see a very long way in all directions. The country is full of these eskers. The trees are growing more and more sparse now.

The day was cloudy and cold, but fitted the mode of the country. A little elevation like this esker makes a big view in this country as it is relatively flat everywhere else. There is something fantastically beautiful in looking at that expanse of desolate, barren country. Here I could get a sense of what land I am in, instead of just seeing a little from the river. Traveling in a group too takes one's mind off the country a great deal. I don't know what it is that makes a man want to travel all over the land that he can see though he knows that it must be pretty much the same everywhere. There is nothing I would rather do than set out with a light pack and a rifle, live off the country as much as possible, and walk all over this land. I don't like the river travel as much as going by foot. The big trees and the ground cover on this esker remind me very much of the Sierras.

After having lunch here, we shoved off down the river, aiming to camp on the esker at Boyd Lake. Tyrrell mentions in his journal that the shores are shallow far out, making them hard to approach by canoe. This makes the eskers the best place to camp. We went on down through little sections of fast water and small lakes with current. As we neared Boyd, we came to some bad rapids. The first of these is a narrow channel between rocky hills with big waves. We shot right through the middle, swinging to the right at the end to avoid some rocks at the tail. About another 100 yards along, we ran another short rapid on the left, avoiding waves in the middle. Then we went on about 1 mi. and camped at the head of the last rapid into Boyd. The country approaching Boyd is all rocky, rounded hills.

Skip | JULY 31, DUBAWNT RIVER

Heavy overcast, strong NW wind and 47F temp greeted us this morning and finally induced us to remain in camp all day. This particular region (according to Tyrrell) is the distinct zone of transition between trees, temperate topography and the real Barrens. Before this we have seen patches of barren land, but it was always interrupted by the scattered return of the trees. Within a few miles we may be in the true Barrens.

Art and I both kept our eyes skyward all day hoping for a brief break in the clouds so that we might photograph this unique area of transitional vegetation, but no luck. Somehow we have to record this region as a pivotal point in the entire metamorphosis of land, flora and fauna; perhaps tomorrow.

We have been out for well over a month and although in normal circumstances this would not be very long, in terms of our isolation, our limited food and strenuous life, it is quite a long period and the effects of the strain are beginning to show. The problem of catching fish and then cleaning and cooking them became a major issue today. Pete and Bruce caught the fish; Pete refusing to clean them; Bruce, George and I cleaned them; George refusing to skin or scale; then whoosh! an argument developed into a battle between George and me concerning the motives of each party member . . . whether we are to be individual or group directed. We argued in general terms, thereby avoiding some antagonism, but the issue remains. He maintains that every one must look out for themselves and thus, indirectly, the group will prosper most effectively. I countered that in our present situation where so much depends on unity, we cannot leave positive group dynamics to individual chance. We must be collectively motivated; that this is a matter of survival, not philosophical nit-picking. We ended agreeing to disagree.

On the brighter side, I caught my first grayling today; fine jumpy, fighty fish, but a great big lake trout is still my favorite; calories prevail!

We are camped in the midst of blueberry heaven. Walking through the laden bushes reminds me of those portages in Quebec where Mom and Dad and I were forever wandering off the trail in search of a bigger, sweeter handful.

Tonight, we had a big meal of glop and blueberry bannock in anticipation of a long day tomorrow, to try and make up for today.

Skip | AUGUST 1, BOYD LAKE

Rose this morning at 6 AM and while breakfast was cooking, I watched the grey overcast sweep away to the West and a perfectly clear, light blue northern sky take over.

Spent 3 hrs., 9–12 PM, making a film sequence of shooting the rapids into Boyd Lake: panoramic shot of the entire rapid from the cliff shore, close ups of faces watching the canoes; three stern men discussing route;

Tyrrell

[W]e paddled over to the high point two miles north-west of camp. . . . The point is a long sloping ridge 150 feet high . . . on its crest is a large boulder, nine feet high. . . . On top of this boulder we erected a cairn of stones, under which we put a Worcestershire sauce bottle, with a short record of our trip to that time, and a sketch map of the course followed.

Lunch break at a small pocket beach, vicinity Boyd Lake.
Courtesy Creigh Moffatt.

side view of shooting canoe from a very low angle behind big waves. Then paddled into the island-dotted lake where we stopped again for a few shots in brilliant sunlight.

Back again into the rhythm of lake travel . . . dip, push; dip, push . . . Trees have disappeared for most practical purposes . . . firewood becomes the object of very passionate scavenger hunts; twisted stumps and water-soaked driftwood are treasures.

Incidentally, it occurred to me that my last bath must have been over 2 weeks ago . . . socks are getting crusty, but I'm still just as sweet!

The terrain is now studded with small, rocky, barren hills, one of which includes our camp. The rocks as well as the ground are covered with varieties of predominantly grey lichens forming a rather gloomy, severe landscape. Some of these hills remind me of old, dilapidated New England cemeteries. From a distance, the lichens resemble clipped grass and the rocks could certainly mark the moldy remains of our dear forefathers.

Perhaps the sunshine and glare . . . perhaps a touch of constipation . . . at any rate, something caused a headache and generally lousy feeling, making me realize that even the most insignificant decrease in efficiency can become a serious problem for the whole group. Our daily exertion is now just normal, but a minor illness or accident could create a serious situation. Paddling on large, open stretches with the sun always behind us to the left as we did today inspires the feeling that we are steadily heading closer and closer toward the prospect of severe northern weather, and the unpleasant anticipation of hardship looms nearer and nearer.

Peter | AUGUST 1, BOYD LAKE

Up at 6:30. Cold and cloudy at first, but cleared off to a fine, warm day. Art is going wild with his movie camera. He set up high in the right bank to get Skip going through the rapid. Then he got down next to the water so as to make the waves look big when I went through. I had no trouble at all. The current went straight through the channel and though it was narrow, I had no trouble in it.

Boyd Lake was quite calm and we had no trouble paddling. We stopped at a sandy spot, perhaps the first esker marked on the map, for lunch. Breaking into the case of peanut butter, we found two jars out of twelve broken. Art took more movies of us paddling after lunch. While I was waiting for Art to get through with the movies, I had a peculiar experience of memory that has happened more and more often in the past year. I remembered certain scenes and especially feelings of my early childhood at San Marino and San Mateo with painful clarity. Painful because they made me long for them and the happiness I had then and yet I know I can never have them again.

The people and places are all gone and changed forever, as I myself have changed. I had a feeling of intense homesickness with no home to return to. No place to rest and call home. Maybe this comes from being away from my parents and sisters for so long, almost nine months now, but they have all changed too. I have a need for close personal relations, but no way to find them as I seem to repel everyone and remain aloof, rather than try to get close to them. Now I am just like an old man hoarding memories of happy times within the family that are all gone. It seems almost impossible that I should ever love some girl enough to have the same feelings. I am too afraid of them and I try too hard to be something besides myself; but perhaps these problems will work themselves out in time. As it is now, I don't feel at home or at rest anywhere or with anyone. I never quite know what to do with myself or how to act with other people.

We paddled on about four hours from where we had lunch and camped on a small horseshoe-shaped island in the narrow part of the lake where it is supposed to be the limit of trees according to the map, but there is still a fringe of trees close to the water's edge. Beyond this, the islands and the shore rise as bare low hills with a ground cover of lichens, Labrador tea and carpet-like stunted plants. Art got some shots of making camp, but some long wispy clouds coming from the south began to cover the sun during dinner. It is still fairly warm, but the sky to the south looks ominous. There was a fantastic sunset. I tried to get some shots of it, but was probably not very successful.

The screws are starting to come out of my soles again. I hope they last another month.

Skip | AUGUST 2, BOYD LAKE

Woke this morning to howling wind and pattering rain . . . rolled over and didn't crawl out of the sack until called for breakfast at 11 AM . . . cook's day off!

Spent the usual wind-bound day, highlighted by Art's catching a tremendous 15# lake trout right off the camp. Just as I was in the middle of a rare warm-water face wash, a yell from the nearby rocks, "Skip, bring the camera! Bring the camera!" I dropped the soap, grabbed the camera and went bounding through the brush onto the rocks and set up the camera and tripod, getting some terrific shots of Art landing the monster, complete with a final, bloody death struggle between fish and fisherman when the line broke and Art pinned the beast with a full-body press. Sequence ended with butchering and a bountiful dinner of fish, mashed pots, bacon and tea.

Peter | AUGUST 2, BOYD LAKE

I awoke to rain on the tent. I feel some pain in my stomach, lower in my intestines; perhaps I did get a few chips of broken glass in the peanut butter I ate yesterday. Only time will tell.

Tyrrell

During the next few days . . . several bad rapids impeded our progress, and we followed the winding shores of several small lakes . . . Patches of snow on the sides of the surrounding hills now remind us that we had reached a sub-arctic region.

We ate breakfast in a gloomy mood with a slow drizzle of rain down our necks. I think I will really regret losing my poncho later on when there is no fire to dry out by. I tried to do a little fishing, but with no success. Joe found some large bear tracks on the island.

I am really beginning to get worried that we will run out of food before we get to Baker Lake. We aren't moving today, though the rain is very slight and the wind not too heavy. After lunch, Art caught a huge lake trout fishing from the shore with a Dare Devil, 39" long, 15.5 lb. Then he caught one about half that size and we had enough for a fish dinner.

That night, while I was walking on top of the high hill before going to bed, I found a perfect arrowhead, long and narrow, notched at the base for tying into the shaft.

Skip | AUGUST 3, BOYD LAKE

Anticipation of a days traveling dragged a somewhat weary breakfast cook out of the sack at 7 AM in spite of a windblown tent and slight rain. Oats, fried fish and tea for breakfast and then the chilling continuation of wind-bound weather. With one or two exceptions, we have not had any real driving rain storms; instead, a monotonous windblown drizzle with the temperature remaining close to 40F.

Only consolation for our stay here is that this lake is full of large lake trout which seem to be spawning and are feeding close to shore so that we can catch them on a Dare Devil. This is a big help to our supply inventory in as much as we have about 45 days of food left and we estimate it will take us at least that long to reach Baker Lake. Stay-over days consume food, but don't decrease mileage and so on days like this we have ½ ration oats + fish, fish chowder for lunch which only needs a package of dried soup and a little milk with boiled chunks of fish; and then fried fish and mashed potatoes for dinner.

The day drags by with a group of wet, disappointed men huddled around a sputtering fire. As I write (5 PM), occasional patches of sunlight appear in the clouds, perhaps forecasting a break up, in which case we will probably break camp after dinner and travel most of the night, stopping late tomorrow afternoon. I'll try to get some sleep now to fortify a long evening paddle.

9:30 PM. We have decided against night travel this evening in spite of clearing skies due to the difficulties of navigating among the many islands of this lake; instead we plan to get up at 4:30 AM and get in as many miles as possible when and if the sun shines.

During dinner today, Art brought up the condition of the supplies and distance to travel, and for the first time made everyone collectively conscious of our situation. We discussed the possibility of returning to Stony Rapids before it was too late, but were agreed to a man to continue, with the definite intention of longer, more strenuous travel days. The

Fish Chowder

Boil gutted fish; remove bones, head, tail, etc.
Boil 3 c diced potatoes, or any other dehy. veggie.
Fry ¼ lb. bacon; break into pieces.
Crisp chopped onion in bacon fat.
Mix above in pot with drippings.
Pour in 1 can evap. milk or use amount of mixed powder milk.
Season with salt, pepper.
Just before chowder comes to boil, add 1 can tomato paste.
Stir and simmer until ready to eat.

attitude of the party finally is changing from that of a leisurely summer vacation to the serious determination of an expedition faced with an urgent objective, and serious consequences if it fails.

Peter | AUGUST 3, BOYD LAKE

Rainy and windy. We decided to stay put for a while. Art and I made a thorough search of the island, but could find no more artifacts besides those on the hill. This must have been a workshop of sorts. It had lots of fragments of white quartz scattered around, but the points that we found were all of a coarse gray or brown quartzite. We found several more points, all broken and in fragments.

By dinner it was still fairly rainy, so we decided to go to bed early and get up at 4:30 tomorrow no matter what the weather. Art seems very worried about our slow pace. Tonight he asked if any of us would consider turning back, but no one wanted to. We are not yet halfway, but we have consumed more than half of supplies.

Skip | AUGUST 4, DUBAWNT RIVER

My day began at 4 AM with cold, wet breakfast preparations. By 6:30 we were loaded; shoved off in a mounting drizzle . . . Temp. 44F. For the next 4 hours, we paddled in cold wind and rain. The dull ache of cramped wetness and shivering cold slowly seeped into me until I could no longer control the spasmodic shuddering that passed through me. Only the faint warmth and rhythmic dullness of paddling kept us going. To add to this misery, we were lost in a haze of islands, groping for an opening out of the lake to the river; the uncertainty and discomfort were immense.

Around 11 AM the rain eased and we pulled into shore under some over-hanging scrub and built an enormous fire. We brewed a pot of cocoa and slowly dried and warmed ourselves. In an hour or so we were back to normal and with the lifting sky could look forward somewhat optimistically to the rest of the day. The conviction grows that this kind of discomfort is a relatively short-lived experience and that determined endurance usually prevails. We are elastic enough to very quickly forget past discomfort and revive in the relief of a comfortable present.

Somewhat reluctantly we left the fire and continued paddling. The country has now definitely evolved into the treeless Barrens and the rocky, gently rolling ridges spread over the entire landscape, forming a series of plains-like skylines.

An hour or two later as we rounded a curve, two buck caribou were seen silhouetted majestically on the ridge directly before us. Their huge "U"-shaped antlers and shaggy white-brown coats contrasted sharply with the light-colored clouds and seemed to intensify the importance of these animals. From that moment on the land seemed to erupt with life. Actually, everywhere we looked groups of caribou could be seen. The horizon was a constant panorama of moving bodies and antlers. The small fawns and indulgent mothers were feeding peacefully along the shore while the bucks remained more distant and perhaps somewhat aloof but just as unconcerned of the silent intruders. Bruce and I approached two caribou in the water and paddled along side for a while, watching the powerful, heaving animals with uplifted heads and fear-rolling eyes.

We soon came to the large rapid at the entrance to Barlow Lake and made camp. The fishing is excellent; the rapids roar in turbulent whiteness, and everywhere the caribou pass by; the more curious stop . . . almost walking through our camp. Such a sudden change from the lifelessness of just a few days before to this swarming migration is magnificent to see. The sun is slow to sink, the flies are temporarily gone, the land pulses with life and vastness, and I go to sleep brim full of positive feelings and excitement for tomorrow.

Peter | AUGUST 4, DUBAWNT RIVER

Up at 4:30. Beautiful red sunrise, then it clouded over and set into rain by the time that we were in the canoes. Cold, about 42 degrees and raining all the while we were paddling through Boyd Lake. It stopped when we got into the river again and we pulled up and built a fire to dry off. I was sure miserable. My wool pants were soaked through, but my upper body was dry. The surplus parka stopped the rain all right, though it was soaked on the outer layer.

We went on down the river through a few small rapids when we saw our first caribou calmly grazing on top of a high bank. Art pulled up and ran up like a wild man with his camera but they were gone by the time he got to the hilltop. When Tyrrell went down, he didn't see caribou until Carey Lake, but we saw them 20 mi. before Barlow Lake. He found one immense herd. We saw many caribou today, but all scattered along the banks in small groups. The horns are still in velvet; even the cows have short prong horns. The calves are abundant this time of year, ranging from dog sized up to colt sized. It was an overwhelming event to see this barren land suddenly running over with big game. We even headed off a couple that were swimming the river and got so close to them in the canoes, we could have killed them with a spear. The caribou really make this trip an experience, along with the country, which is getting quite barren and rocky now with small patches of stunted spruce.

We made camp above a big rapid that sweeps around to the left and Art went out to get pictures of the caribou. I caught a few grayling for breakfast, then climbed a hill to look at the country. It is full of long, low hills, barren for the most part, but green with ground cover of grass and moss. The country is dotted with lakes. We will probably stay here tomorrow and get a caribou for fresh meat. There are several herds of about fifty or less around here.

Tyrrell, 1893	Location	Moffatt, 1955
July 29–August 2	Carey Lake	August 7–8

Skip | AUGUST 5, DUBAWNT RIVER

Spent the day in camp and although the weather was poor for filming, the caribou offered plenty of opportunity for excitement. After breakfast, Bruce and Joe climbed a nearby ridge, picked out a young, spike horn and shot it. None of us had ever had any experience in skinning and butchering such a large animal (squirrels being just about the limit of our experience), but with much blood and gore, George and I managed, primarily by trial and error, to produce a good quantity of serviceable meat. The prospect of firm, chewable meat for the next few days is very welcome.

It is interesting to note the different standards of "game morality" which I seem to possess. At home, in the absence of real need, I am critical of the urban hunter who annually participates in what I think of as a contrived tradition of "sportsmanship" and manliness. But here an entire change of attitude prevails. Fish, caribou, grouse, ptarmigan, ducks . . . all are hunted with determination and ruthlessness. The only morality exists in terms of non-waste and need. As long as the herds are with us, we will kill individual animals as needed; eat as much meat as possible immediately and carry whatever we can. This sudden presence of wildlife not only provides good protein and some fat, it also makes the hope of adequate provisions more realistic.

Peter | AUGUST 5, DUBAWNT RIVER

Slept for more than twelve hours last night. No one got up 'til noon. We had all the grayling we could eat for breakfast, then Bruce and Joe went off with their rifles to get a caribou, followed by Art and his camera. I took off for a long walk. I headed inland for a couple of miles and then struck a long lake and walked up the shore several miles toward a hill of gray rock. The shore parallels the river closely and is only about a mile from it. When I first struck this lake, I found a quartzite scraper on top of a hill, then walking along the shore, I found a perfect, beautifully worked arrowhead in the middle of a caribou trail. Only the tip was broken off; the rest was in perfect shape. The land between the river and the lake is covered with bare sandy spots with lots of quartzite chips.

In the lake there was a low island about in the middle, and caribou use this to help them cross the lake, swimming from one shore to the island and from the island to the other shore. I watched a large herd swim across this way. Caribou are abundant everywhere. They warn themselves chiefly by smell, so by standing downwind of a small group and remaining quite still, I found that they would graze very close without noticing me.

Before I climbed the rock hill, I found a few big white spruce, the trunks about 1.5 ft. through at the base. The view I got from this hilltop was the best yet. I could see Barlow Lake to the northeast. The country looks flatter in that direction with not much rock exposed and fairly green. It reminded me of some of the high Sierras very far above timberline. All gray rock and every so often a lake without a bit of grass or growing stuff anywhere. A moon world! I got a feeling of loneliness and desolation and was glad to get down and back on my way back to camp. The water below is full of grayling, all good sized and eager for the fly.

Back in camp, I found that Bruce and Joe had shot a young female. They did a very poor job, riddled the meat with bullets, but at least we have all the meat we want.

Everyone sits up at night broiling it and eating 'til they can hold no more. The best pieces are the long roasts from the back. They are very tender and delicious. No gamey flavor at all, except for the bloody taste of fresh meat.

Skip | AUGUST 6, BARLOW LAKE

Spent the entire day on the river, battling the wind which swept across the valley, building large, confused waves as it blew against the current. Rapids were very difficult to negotiate as sudden gusts of wind upset the balance and heading of the canoe and drove the waves in an unpredictable cross chop. Also came very close to hitting a few big rocks, but fortunately they were far enough below the surface.

Pan-fried steaks replaced yesterday's delicious dinner stew and for the second evening in a row, we enjoy fresh meat.

The abundance of caribou has already ceased to be cause for comment as we pass herd after herd along the river.

In the evening after the meal, a leisurely stroll over the open, rocky ridges reveals hundreds of caribou peacefully grazing and only moving when we are within 20–30 ft. or so. The antlers are still in velvet; the broad branching U of the male with one or two shovels over the forehead contrasts sharply with the smaller U of the female. Body size is not such a distinguishing feature as it is with deer or elk. They vary in color from dark brown to grey-white and have a slight hump on the shoulder. They stride with a bouncing step; generally beginning with a slight hop or leap; then throwing back their head and moving off with a deceptively rapid gait. As they run, the ankle bones produce a rattling click with each step and often during the night, we can hear the eerie echo of these rattling hooves as the caribou wander by our tents.

I am sitting on a high, exposed ridge just above our riverbank camp. The wind has died and the sun is still quite high. As I write, Peter and Bruce have stirred up a few caribou just north of me and in their haste the animals run within 15 ft of the rock on which I am sitting . . . the young docilely following the females, with the vigilant males in front and on the flank. They run for a while, stop, look back; graze a bit and then move on . . . always southward.

My view from here stretches for miles in every direction. Tiny lakes exposed between the ridges; still patches of dwarfed spruce, and always the lichen-covered rocks and stunted, inch-high ground cover stretching forever.

Although the day was quite clear, the atmosphere possesses a strange haze which seems to be common here. And, of course, to remind us of our position and direction, bright sunshine still means 3 layers of shirts, cold hands and tingling feet.

Peter | AUGUST 6, BARLOW LAKE

Started off at the usual early time, 6 AM. Art got some good pictures of us running the rapid and then we went down the river to Barlow Lake. The country is continuing to get more barren as we go on with less and less trees along the bank. The river is quite swift and we made pretty good time. The weather has certainly improved. A warm, sunny day, but lots of wind.

Before we got to Barlow, we went through a small, shallow lake. Coming from this into Barlow, the river is very shallow and rocky, but not too swift. I am having lots of trouble with George. He just won't do as I tell him and in one bad spot, he refused to do anything and just sat down his paddle. Fortunately, we got through this shallow part okay and after paddling a few miles on Barlow, we camped on a point with a high hill and a beautiful view of the lake.

I found a rose quartzite scraper in fine shape, well made. Art got some movies of me finding it and holding it to the camera for a close-up.

We had caribou steaks cut from the meat along the back and they were as tender as the finest filet mignon. Another good piece is any of the largest muscles on the hind legs.

Skip | AUGUST 7, CAREY LAKE

Enjoyed a full day of clear, sunny weather while traversing the entire length of Barlow Lake and five miles of river into Carey Lake; pushed along by a rare, gentle south wind.

We have become used to the stepped-up tempo of 6 AM breakfasts so that by 9 AM pictures have been taken, canoes loaded and we are off.

At dinner tonight, Art by very illogical reasoning insisted that the dinner cook should be entitled to extra sugar rations. He seems to be suffering more than the rest of us from the short rations due mainly to large amounts of coffee and tea that he relishes, but I certainly thought he would be the last to hedge. After I refused him in an ashamed and disappointed way, he dropped the subject and has not mentioned it since.

Perhaps the incident was just a momentary weakness to which we all are entitled, but he above all should set an example of steady discipline.

Caribou meat continues to dominate our meals; tongue and heart are top delicacies.

Shipped about 3" of water while shooting rapids today; late in the afternoon, tired, mistake in judgment. None of the supplies got wet.

Peter | AUGUST 7, CAREY LAKE

A good, clear warm day; no wind to speak of. We finished the rest of Barlow Lake. There is one swift rapid with bad waves out of Barlow. Skip ran this first, going on the outside of some white water close to the shore in the mid-portion, but the current carried him off course through some of the biggest waves and he nearly swamped. Then I went down, going close to the left shore inside this part of white water, then swinging out from the shore to avoid some heavy waves at the tail. We made it with no water at all. Art took the same course, but shipped a lot of water and had to bail. He is heavier loaded now, though we were the heaviest at the beginning of the trip.

After this rapid, there are two more easy ones and then just swift water in to Carey Lake. Carey looks really barren after you pass a few spruce at the inlet, but so did most of Barlow. The trees don't seem to follow a definite pattern, but by now they are all confined to small patches that occur apparently at random.

We camped here at the inlet; still eating on our caribou. We tried smoking some and eating it for lunch and it turned out delicious. I think the meat gets better as it ages a little. Caribou have been getting scarcer since we saw a big herd on the river before Barlow. Since then, we have only been seeing the odd one or two, all fairly far away.

Skip | AUGUST 8, DUBAWNT RIVER

Was awakened this morning by a nearby wolf howl. We were camped on the w shore of a ¼-mile-wide bay, and as I crawled out of the tent,

Skip Pessl and Joe Lanouette collecting driftwood and small willow twigs for the evening cook fire, Dubawnt River vicinity Barlow-Carey Lakes. Courtesy Creigh Moffatt.

I saw two large white wolves wandering on the opposite shore among the rocks. Through the glasses the long, low-slung bodies with beautiful white fur and drooping tails were pretty big, much larger than a German Shepherd, and built for agility and power. By the time Art was up and ready to film they were gone. Hope to get good shots of them another time.

The threatening skies of early morning soon cleared and we spent a sunny, calm day traversing the entire length of Carey Lake.

Stopped at the site of Tyrrell's cairn for lunch, but were disappointed to find only a note from a survey party this Spring . . . they cheat with airplanes.

Got a very rare shot of a long-tailed Jaeger on a rocky island in mid-lake.

Latest fad finds us all preparing half-smoked, half-cooked meat after the evening meal to supplement the lunch ration . . . caribou of course. First animal is running out; will be looking for a new kill soon.

Saw first ptarmigan today, but these were much too shy to get for the pot . . . more to come.

With the favorable change in the weather, we have been making good progress, 50 mi. in 3 days and the prospects of early arrival at Baker Lake seem good.

Peter | AUGUST 8, DUBAWNT RIVER

Again, a pretty clear day. Art saw a pair of white Arctic wolves across the river this morning, but so far away they were just little specks. We got up at the usual time, 6 AM and were moving by 9:30. The lake was calm and we made good time to Cairn Point. Actually there is no big cairn, just a large boulder like the other erratics. This one happens to be on the way.

We climbed to the top of the hill, found the site of Tyrrell's cairn and a note in a glass jar that a survey crew of May '55 had left. We signed our names on the back of this; all but mine. I was wandering around looking at the view.

Carey from here is a picture of loneliness, almost as complete as what I saw to the west from the hills I climbed by Barlow. The hills around are low and grassy, but completely barren. To the east, the country is flatter and swampy with hills in the far distance. The panorama is so immense that it is impossible to really take it in. You keep looking for something that isn't there. It makes me want to go off on a long trip across country, but what I see there will be no different from this part. These barrens make me want to spread myself too thin.

We ate lunch at this point, then headed out for the gap at the left side of the lake. When we got through this, we headed for the large point of land on the right shore that shows up as a big hill in the distance. While passing through the little rocky islands along the way, Art got some pictures of jaeger, supposedly a very rare bird and hard to photograph.

When we got past the point, we headed for the little rocky islands off it, going through shallow, rocky water with current. Then we came out into the last section of the lake and paddled down to the first rapids. We camped at the head of the rapids on the right, which we would have to portage the next day. An easier way, if possible, is to shoot the first rapids on the left side of the island and go around that way. I know the first is not too hard, but the other around the left side might have to be portaged. We had to wade the canoes through boulders to get to the right shore.

We had our last meal from the caribou tonight, but the chuck is still left and is good, except for tough membrane on the outside of the meat. Once the meat is broiled or fried, this membrane becomes soft enough so it doesn't interfere much.

Skip | AUGUST 9, DUBAWNT RIVER

After portaging around the rapids at which we camped last night and having completed a very cold, wet-foot loading job, we continued down the river for a mile or so, only to be stopped by north winds and threatening sky; total mileage not more than a few miles.

Sugar again became an issue this morning with Art "borrowing" from the cooking ration. Later he apologized for the infraction and all seems smooth again.

Berry picking led me to within a few feet of a caribou this afternoon. As I crouched among the rocks, she sauntered over toward me and lay down quite contentedly to chew; reminded me of Rigo* arranging a place to settle down. Other than the big bucks, the individual caribou are rather bedraggled and seem quite forlorn among the vastness of the Barrens.

Peter | AUGUST 9, DUBAWNT RIVER

We made the portage around the first rapid, about ⅓ mi. over quite open country. I flushed five ptarmigan in one trip over. Right around this rapid is the first that we have seen of them, but they are certainly in abundance here. I didn't try hunting them, but I should think it might be difficult to get a clear shot.

The loading was bad again here. The rocks are all sharp and rough and

*The family dog.

shallow close into shore. Today is very windy with a few thunderstorms galloping about.

Due to Art getting pictures of portaging and ptarmigan, we didn't start loading until 11:30. Then it was so windy that we decided not to shoot the next few rapids, though they were fairly easy. While looking over the rapids, we left our canoes tied in the lee of a point and they scraped against some of the sharp rocks. Result, Skip's canoe had several bad scrapes down to bare canvas and one hole right through to the wood. Mine had one big scrape to canvas about 4" long. I never would have thought a little gentle rubbing and scraping could be so hard on that tough paint and canvas, but these rocks were sharp and cut right through. Skip patched the hole with tar. I used a liquid cement to keep the canvas from rotting.

We holed up for the rest of the day and I slept most of the afternoon. Caribou are getting quite scarce with only an occasional one showing up.

Skip | AUGUST 10, DUBAWNT RIVER

Made good progress this morning, running four rapids . . . the first decision to run or not is still with me; so far so good.

Storm-bound in an abandoned trapper's cabin just south of Markham Lake.

This cabin is quite an amazing thing to see so far from other signs of civilization. The floor plan must be about 8' x 8' with one genuine glass window approx. 18" x 18" and a small overhanging porch. A crude, square tin stove is in one corner, a single bunk in the opposite corner. The door clears about 6" off the rough planked floor. A small shelf is built on the wall next to the window and opposite this, the entire wall is covered with nets and traps hung from hand-whittled pegs. The walls are made of 8"–12" white spruce squared on all sides; must have hauled them from a small stand of stunted trees in a valley to the south. Wall chinking is moss. The roof is made of small split logs, chinked with moss and then covered with gravel, bottles and old canoe canvas. Dog stakes and hand-made wooden implements are scattered around outside. These implements and the interior of the cabin especially emphasize the builder's ingenuity and ability to fashion necessities out of things on hand; must be a tough, challenging experience to spend a winter in such a place.

The six of us sit here, brewing tea, listening to the rain and speculate on what manner of man the owner was . . . Art measures the cabin and speculates; George holds forth on the hypocrisy of hermits; Joe rolls cigarettes; Pete reads a dime novel found in a wooden box; Bruce agrees and marks the map.

I don't understand why the cabin was built on such an exposed ridge for, although the door opens to the south, the cabin is completely exposed to 3–4 barren miles of north wind; perhaps to see game from a comfortable vantage point, and there are lots of caribou here today.

Left this mysterious place after the weather cleared and we paddled under a beautiful sunny sky in anticipation of reaching Markham Lake.

This region has a lot of exposed bedrock in the form of steep cliffs along the river and somewhat higher distant hills. In the brilliant sunlight of this afternoon, our view of the dark water meeting the multicolored rocks under a light blue sky with white, fluffy clouds was a beautiful sight and inspired a feeling of comfort and compatibility with the country. At times like this, it seems that nothing can go wrong, everything is perfect; and yet we know the unpredictability of this land and the elements.

Peter | AUGUST 10, DUBAWNT RIVER

Calm, but thunderheads are still rolling around on the horizon. We made a good early start and shot a few easy rapids before coming to one big one. The maps are very inaccurate in placing the rapids for the most part. This one was long, easy at the top, but with one stretch at the bottom which is rocky and has big waves. We took the left side to the end, then went through the middle, just skimming the right side of a large exposed rock at the very end. It looked bad, but was actually not too hard.

After this big rapid, the river is calm and wide for a ways. We saw more caribou today, but still only singles and pairs.

The country all around the river is hilly and rough with big chunks of rock thrusting through the surface till here and there. After coming into a wide, calm stretch, we found a cabin perched on a low hill next to the water. A small affair, 9' x 9', built out of square hewn logs notched to fit. The logs were pretty big and must have come from a good-sized spruce grove up the river. No supplies, but a small stove and a bare bunk. The roof was of smaller logs covered with sod and stones. I would like to bring a mountain of supplies and spend a winter in a cabin like this or the one back at Hinde Lake on the esker.

Right now, my thoughts are constantly preoccupied with food to an alarming extent. What I miss is not fresh meat, because we have plenty of that. I crave fats, sugar and starch. I would like big slabs of cornbread with lots of butter, fat meat like bacon or pork, and chocolate. If I ever go on a trip like this again, I would bring my reflector and a lot of unmade starch, such as flour and cornmeal, along with more bacon and some canned butter. Baking for two men is easy; though for six, it really is a chore.

After we had lunch, we stayed in the cabin and sat out a thunderstorm, then moved on down the river. At this time, the clouds cleared away and we found ourselves in a narrow section of river with hills close in on either side. We stopped to look over a rapid and the country was really beautiful. From the hills, you could see the river rushing along into a wide lake-like place. The light was golden and the water dark blue. The rapid was easy running it on the left. I came down first, while Art and Skip took pictures. I kept going and came out on the wide stretch and just sat baking in the sun. We camped half way along the wide area on the right. When Art arrived, he had found the nest of a duck hawk along the way in a cliff along the left shore. We turned in early tonight, as Art has plans to go back and get movies early in the morning.

Skip | AUGUST 11, POND ABOVE MARKHAM LAKE

Got up at 4:30 AM, planning to photograph duck hawks on a nearby cliff at dawn, but a low, mist-like cloud discouraged us from moving until almost 10 AM. Day of rest was declared and while Art and I took pictures, Bruce bagged a caribou and with the help of Pete and George, butchered the beauty. Once again we are well stocked with meat.

The duck hawk which was the objective of most of our morning filming is a very powerful and ferocious bird. It is the bird used by many falconers

Art Moffatt overlooking a duck hawk nest on a bedrock cliff along the Dubawnt River, south of Markham Lake. Courtesy Creigh Moffatt.

and kills by striking its prey with closed claws during flight, breaking the backbone and then catching the falling body before it strikes the ground. The bird has a general gray appearance with faintly striped breast, bluish neck, black cap, yellow legs and dark wings. The pair defended their nest with fierce cries and determined dive bombing, always pulling up just before striking, fortunately; should make a good film sequence.

Blueberries are super and with the meat and fish provide a very substantial part of our diet. This is my first experience with "living off the land," substantially backed up by a can or two as needed. So far so good; shower lessens and glop is served.

Peter | AUGUST 11, POND ABOVE MARKHAM LAKE

Very heavy fog this morning. We had breakfast around 4:30. The fog gradually cleared, but I went back to bed and slept 'til 10:00. By this time, Art and Skip had taken the canoe to get pictures of the hawk. I sat around washing clothes, a beautiful sunny day. Skip came back. We had lunch and he left to go back to Art again.

Then about 2:00 Bruce came in. He had been hunting caribou all morning and finally got a young cow about noon. He had lunch, then he, I and George went back to the kill. Since I wanted the hide to keep me dry in the next bad rain, I did the skinning. It came pretty easy; just a cut down the middle and around the neck and along the inside of the legs. Once you get a hold of the right layer, the skin peels off easily. This time we tried leaving the meat along the back, right on the bone, and taking the ribs back too. There was hardly any of that caribou left when we walked off. The meat is no good for a day after it has been killed, so we hung it and had glop that night, a welcome change from the usual meat. The hide was pretty shabby. The skin along the back was full of bott fly holes and the new hair had not completely come in. The old white winter hair kept falling out at a touch, but it is good enough to keep the rain off my legs when I am in the canoe, so it will serve. I am a bloody mess and so is George, but I guess we will get used to the smell after a bit.

Skip | AUGUST 12, POND ABOVE MARKHAM LAKE

Shortly after breakfast, rain closed in and pushed us to our tents where we dozed, read and wrote until a break in the showers permitted a humid lunch and then back to the tents for more rain-induced sleep. Rain let up in early evening, but too late for travel, so energies were spent preparing a beautiful blueberry johnny cake which was combined with two enormous slabs of "roast beef" to produce a fine banquet. The quantities of meat which we consume at one sitting are enormous; the local A&P would have a hell of a time keeping up with this group.

We sat around the fire until quite late this evening nursing a boiling pot of soup stock made of caribou backbone chopped in chunks, reinforced by the usual pot of tea, hoping to see a predicted meteor shower. But

Johnny Cake

Mix well with enough water to make a fairly heavy batter:

- 2 cups yellow corn meal
- 1 cup all purpose flour
- ½ cup sugar
- 1 tsp salt
- ⅓ cup butter or Crisco
- 1½ tsp baking powder (double action)
- 2 tbs powdered milk

Bake in well-greased reflector pan, 15–20 minutes in medium heat (until batter rises and is clean to a knife)

Brown top by tilting pan in front of fire

Adding berries, raisins or any other fruit to the batter offers change

And if grub is plentiful, brown sugar, honey, or jam furnish fine topping for this luxurious dish.

occasional clouds and the general twilight prevented it from being more than a very few traveling sparks. Later on, when the evening tea invited me out into the chilly night, I was treated with a brilliant picture of an almost-full moon of intense brilliance shinning down from a cloud-swept sky on to the black, rippled waters of this widening in the Dubawnt. No meteors, but wisps of rising steam created an eerie, Hamletesque tone . . . "witches and ghosts" were lurking everywhere. Bright stars peered down through momentary openings in the clouds and seemed to be strange eyes from another world looking in on this fascinating scene.

Peter | AUGUST 12, POND ABOVE MARKHAM LAKE

Rainy all day. We stayed put and I slept and read in the morning and early afternoon. I read Thomas Wolfe's "The Hills Beyond" and looked through George's book of art. Some of the paintings impressed me very much. There is so much you can convey in a painting that would be impossible to express another way. I like the landscapes best. They can convey more of a mood and an outlook on life to me than a portrait. A lot of "Hills Beyond" is in the form of episodes in Wolfe's life; an account of his childhood that rambles along without any plot. I like his descriptions. They reminded me of my own memories of childhood and how freshly and strongly everything affected me. I like too, the obsession he has with the passage of time, because I have often liked to sit and feel time stream on and wonder what it is that we measure out our lives in.

We had a pretty gloomy lunch in the rain, then went back to our tents to wait it out. Around 4:00, the sky cleared and Art set about making a johnny cake. I almost went mad with hunger sitting around watching him, so I went off to pick blueberries. We picked quite a pot full to put in the johnny cake and they really improved the flavor, but the cake itself sits so heavy once you eat two big slabs of it that I almost wished I was hungry again.

Tonight we had a brief display of northern lights, but nothing like what I have seen before at Smooth Stone portage on the Albany.

Skip | AUGUST 13, POND ABOVE MARKHAM LAKE

The usual morning oats under what has become a characteristic gray, morning overcast were supplemented with vast quantities of fried caribou liver to the delight of most of the party. Art and Joe abstained, Art due to taste, Joe in fear of flukes.

By now we have become quite skilled in utilizing most of the kill. The hide is scraped, dried, then pounded and rubbed until soft enough to be worked; hood and lap robe are intended products. The head yields tongue and brain; former boiled and eaten cold, the latter used for softening the hide. Heart and liver are cooked as special delicacies, and then of course all the available meat is butchered and hung on a tripod. Flies, maggots, cists, tapeworms, flukes, etc. generally cease to be a concern.

After the initial "halfway" scare of time-distance regarding remaining food supplies which resulted in a revised, longer-day travel schedule, we are slowly drifting back into our previous lethargy. Tendency is to wait until near-perfect weather before moving and then only after whatever filming opportunities we create, and then to stop whenever rain or wind threaten. In this land of fish, caribou and berries all seems well and so we mosey along. Things will probably change again but for the present it is most enjoyable.

Left camp about 11 AM and paddled a short distance, shot one short rapids; enjoyed caribou soup for lunch, continued for a few miles into the lake until we were forced to seek shelter from a freshening headwind in a wooded bay; are camped again with the sizzle of cooking steaks.

The recent lag in the caribou migration seems to be over, for today we once again saw the animals grazing along the shore like cows, looking up from their munching as we paddled silently by, and then turning idly back to graze. Occasionally a spirited buck would snort and prance along the shore with us for a short distance, tossing his head and waving a magnificent set of antlers, but always with more curiosity than aggression and certainly very little fright.

Clouds close in as dinner is served.

Left to right: George Grinnell, Bruce LeFavour, Joe Lanouette, Peter Franck (standing) with Art Moffatt in his moosehide parka filling his controversial pannikin (journal entry August 14). Courtesy Creigh Moffatt.

Peter | AUGUST 13, POND ABOVE MARKHAM LAKE

Heavy mist again this morning, but it lifted about 9:00. Still it looked like rain, so we stuck around camp for a while. I scraped most of the remaining flesh off my hide and let it dry out. I am not going to bother doing anything else unless I have to. I think it will be soft enough to wear as it is now.

We pulled out at about 10:30 and went on down to where the 15-ft. falls is marked on the map. Actually this is an error. There was nothing there but a very easy rapid. We had a tremendous lunch of the usual hardtack and a soup made by boiling the backbone of the caribou. Delicious soup, and I had had a lot of caribou liver for breakfast, so I was quite full. This liver is excellent, but too rich and filling to eat for breakfast.

We had to wait around after lunch while Art tried to get some pictures. This is what I dislike most about this trip, having to wait around at odd times when you don't have enough time to take a walk or get started on a project of your own. Also I have a pretty hard time with George. He and I just can't get along together and there is nothing to be done about it; "A fundamental conflict of incompatible natures."

When Art got back, on we went another 3 mi. into Markham Lake. Here the headwind got so bad, we had to camp. We only made about 6 mi., but at least we moved.

I am beginning to get a little bit tired of caribou and long for a glop dinner for a change. These blueberries that grow everywhere are delicious, especially with milk and sugar. I notice that Art is getting awfully hoggish on the food. With oats, he fills his pannikin, which is larger than our bowls and gets more that way. He makes himself thick milk for his tea and hides it so we won't use it. He certainly doesn't try to set a high example for the rest of us, but that is like him. He is a completely natural person with no illusions. We all resent it, but it is acknowledged and out in the open, and not sneaky. If all could be known, I am by far the worst offender having stolen so much food on the sly. I don't even try to stop myself now. If I think I can get away with it, I take something.

Skip | AUGUST 14, DUBAWNT RIVER

Fairness is the cardinal virtue. Little things, which normally would pass unnoticed, too often become the basis for mounting resentment under the stress of cramped, limited living. Art, for example, enjoys the position of leader of this party and yet he is invariably involved in every food dispute. He is the target of much grumbling and the cause of dissatisfaction. This is generally brought upon himself by his failure to establish fairness between himself and the others. As cook, he misuses his job in very minor, but noticeable ways. He uses a special aluminum pannikin instead of the common bowl, thus causing suspicion of larger portions. When frying meat, he always fries his separately at the end, thus implying special pieces and extra preparation. He uses community sugar for personal use at times and tends to hedge on rations as part of compensation for cooking. All these things are minor, but in his position are compromising and disruptive.

We crossed both Markham and Nicholson Lakes today under beautiful, sunny, cool sky. The magic word "Dubawnt Lake" looms next.

It is difficult to know just how much of the general plan of a day's travel should be discussed by the group and how much dictated by the leader, especially when depended upon such a variable as weather, but it seems that in either case, majority or dictator, the group works much better when immediate goals are known and understood. Even in cases of change, revisions should be understood. When proposing two alternatives with an obvious personal choice, it remains far better at least initially to state the two choices fairly, rather than trying to phrase the choices in a biased way. The issue simply rests upon consistency and open handedness. Art is not very good at this.

Peter | AUGUST 14, DUBAWNT RIVER

We got up at the usual 6:00, but didn't leave until 10:30. Art took pictures. It looked like a bad day in the morning, but this cleared off by noon and we had hot sun for the rest of the day. The odd clump of trees is getting harder and harder to find. Caribou are getting more abundant for some reason. We have been seeing lots of them since we entered Markham; still not in big herds, but small groups of three or four are common.

We made it up Markham and into Nicholson by 5:00. When entering Nicholson, take the entrance to the left. The one in the middle is too shallow and rocky. The country is full of sweeping vistas of big, bare hills, golden in the sun. We stuck to the left side going inside of the big island on the left and made it to the mouth of the river by 7:30. Fishing is probably good here. I saw quite a few rises.

The stretch of river coming up is about 30 mi., very narrow, rough and fast. Then we are in Dubawnt Lake!

I have an alarming tendency to look forward to lunch and especially a peanut butter and cheese hardtack as the high point of the day. I am beginning to think that when the chips are down, I am nothing but a big belly. I look forward to Baker Lake most because it means all I can eat.

Skip | AUGUST 15, NORTH OF LAKE NICHOLSON

After spending much of the morning stalking and filming a very wily flock of Canada Geese on the far shore of the river, we pushed off and headed down the Dubawnt, toward the great lake. We soon stopped to

Skip Pessl, standing, with Bruce LeFavour approaching a rapids on the Dubawnt River north of Nicholson Lake. Courtesy Creigh Moffatt.

look over two rapids, both of which we decided to run. As I entered the first rapid it became evident that things were not entirely as they had looked from the shore. Instead of the normal waves breaking below the rocks and at right angles to the flow of the channel, these waves were breaking in a confused series of 3 or 4 directions. The rapid was quite short; we continued on to the second. Again, as we entered, the irregular waves seemed to break everywhere. The surprise of finding an unfamiliar situation in what had become a rather familiar challenge combined with the fear of a serious accident to create a sense of helplessness and a call to "Hang on!" The waves grew larger and soon the canoe was being tossed around uncontrollably. My only control was to keep the canoe more or less parallel with the current. She tossed and twisted, buffeted on the stem by one wave, then slapped by two on the stern. One wave came over at the bow and many lapped over amidships. By the time we reached the lower eddy, we crouched in a waterlogged, sluggish canoe and slowly made our way to shore.

Unloading; no supplies lost; and then Bruce and I helped the other two canoes portage. Afterward, we continued down the river much more respectful of the new power and deep strength of the river. We stopped for the night at the head of a heavy rapid flowing between steep rock cliffs.

Peter | AUGUST 15, NORTH OF LAKE NICHOLSON

Up at 6:00; a fairly clear day with a light south wind. After breakfast Art went off with his camera, so I picked blueberries; very ripe now. I walked back to a hill about ⅓ mi. inland. The country reminds me of meadows very high above timberline in the Sierras. The hills are rolling and long with outcroppings of rock and no trees, except for an occasional stunted growth in a gully or by a pond.

Art went out with Skip in a canoe to get pictures of Canada geese, so I had plenty of time to roam around. With the sun out on days like this, the Barrens look friendly and familiar, like hills not far from home, but let the sun go behind a cloud and the wind come up, and they become ominous and a place to hurry through.

We didn't get started 'til 11:30, but made good time in the river until we pulled over to look at the first rapid. There was about a quarter of a mile of swift water above it, but the main rapid is short, steep and narrow; no rocks, but full of bad waves. Skip ran it first, but almost swamped, so Art and I made a short portage around this swift chute. We didn't leave here until about 4:00 and went down the next calm stretch of river about a mile until the river narrowed down and got very swift heading into a deep gorge. Here we pulled aside on the right and walked down a half mile or more to look. This one is very bad. The water is too swift to stop anywhere much lower than where we stopped, but it is all easily runnable until you get right in the gorge, then the waves are very big and break in all directions. A portage from where we are now might be too long to be practical. We decided to stay put for the night and take a closer look the next day.

This caribou seems to be going bad much faster than the other. It already smells high and some pieces are full of maggots.

Caribou seem to be increasing. We see them all the time now, right close to camp.

Art tried to get pictures of a pair of American rough-legged hawks in this gorge tonight before dinner, but couldn't; not enough sun. After dinner, we saw two mink climbing through the rocks and looking at us not 10 yd. from camp.

Skip | AUGUST 16, DUBAWNT RIVER

We spent the entire morning scouting this very difficult rapid which involved rough walking through low brush and on steep cliffs for over two miles. We looked at the large breaking waves and sharp curves for hours, plotting and replotting possible courses. The wind and pulsating current seems to shift the waves continuously, making any decision tenuous at best. Returned to camp with two plans and finally decided on the alternative of shooting to the left bank into an eddy, lining the canoes down to another eddy, portaging behind the cliff and around difficult curves, and then shooting the last part of the main rapid. The protection of our supplies dictates our caution.

Decided to eat lunch before starting off at which time a sudden squall from the south inclined us to repitch the tents and wait out the rain. Cleared about 4:30; however, have decided to remain in camp until tomorrow. The tension between scouting and making a decision about a rapid, and our awareness of the approaching winter is a huge burden on days like this. Smooth lake travel is a luxury even though much slower and more laborious.

Milk became an issue yesterday; and again it seemed to be the four guys against Art; problem of rationing given to Skip.

After a touchy trial and error mushroom test in which I gulped down one raw specimen with some misgiving, but with no immediate after effects, mushrooms have become part of our "natural" diet. They are very plentiful in this area and when fried in bacon grease are a fine supplement with the caribou steaks.

Food from the land has become so important that everyone walks with head down and a sharp eye for berries, mushrooms and other edible plants. An unfortunate result of this is that thoughts of food seem to dominate almost all other mental activity. Conversation, spare time and imagination concentrate on food. This is a sad state of affairs, considering generally how well we eat.

Peter | AUGUST 16, DUBAWNT RIVER

It looked like a pretty fair day. In the morning after breakfast, Skip and I walked all the way down and took a careful look at the rapid. Art, who had looked at it before breakfast, thought we couldn't shoot the whole thing and the best thing to do would be to shoot the upper part and pull over in the small eddy on the left bank before the bad waves, portage this part, and set in another eddy further down, shooting the bottom part on the left side. Skip and I still thought we could shoot the whole thing. Besides, the eddy on the left was very rocky and hard to get into with the current going past at a terrific rate. While we were talking this over and eating lunch, a bad thunderstorm came up and we spent the rest of the afternoon in the tents.

Around 4:00 the rain stopped and Bruce and I got out and caught some fish. The rapid is full of grayling and lake trout; fine big fish, the fattest I have ever seen. We had a caribou stew and threw the rest away as it was too high to stand any longer.

After dinner, Art got out the maps and looked over our situation. It seems rather serious. We still have 300 mi. to Baker Lake, after we get to Dubawnt Lake and only about thirty days of food left. The weather will be getting worse all the time and there is no telling how long we will be held up on Dubawnt Lake from storms. I have given up all hope of getting to college on time. I am worried about getting out of the bush before winter starts closing in. The people back at Stony said this was an early summer. Perhaps that means it will end early too? Tyrrell had freezing weather by September 20th. Art thinks that the river may be lower now than when Tyrrell went through as Tyrrell didn't have much trouble with any of these rapids. The ice at Spring breakup can change things a lot in seventy-five years too.

I feel unsettled and anxious mostly because I don't have the clothes to stand the cold, if it does come. I doubt that my boots will last another thirty days. I am going to try to save a little hardtack each day from now on so that I will have something to fall back on, if things do go badly.

Skip | AUGUST 17, DUBAWNT RIVER

Stayed in bed as long as possible today while one of the rare driving rains made the tent a very cozy place. Breakfast of oats, lake trout, bacon, blueberries and tea was eaten in a heavy rain by the six of us huddled under the tarp, close around a smoky, sputtering fire.

Skies cleared in the afternoon, but storms continued to threaten so we remained at camp and spent most of the day getting food so as not to use much of our rapidly diminishing store-bought supply.

Lunch consisted of a fish chowder utilizing 5 grayling, 1 C rice and 1 pkg. dried soup; also 1 hardtack with jam. Dinner was really a woodsman's triumph, although it took all afternoon to gather. Five medium lake trout which we catch at will are served as the main course. A large bucket of mushrooms was fried for our vegetable and blueberries furnished dessert along with the customary tea.

Later in the evening Pete came in with 3 ptarmigan which are hanging on a tent pole now and will serve as the beginning of another meal soon.

In addition to saving on supplies, these "land meals" are teaching me many things. Butchering the caribou, preparing birds, picking and cooking mushrooms and, of course, preparing the fish have all become ordinary chores and will always be useful. It is marvelous and quite fortunate how abundant food in the Barrens is at this season and how six quite inexperienced men are able to supply a substantial part of their diet with such ease.

The recent hot weather has ruined a lot of our meat so that even boiling the worst parts is no longer too effective. However, a change to fish for a while is welcome.

Mink play on the rocky shore within a few feet of our camp; energetic, sleek little animals.

The big rapid still remains a problem. Hope we can tackle it tomorrow.

Clouds and coming winter have pretty well done away with the pleasant, leisurely twilight camp hours. I am writing now by candle light in the tent and enjoy the meager warmth as well as the light.

Peter | AUGUST 17, DUBAWNT RIVER

Awoke to the sound of heavy rain on the tent, so I just went back to sleep again. We finally had breakfast in the rain about 10:00. Then I did the dishes and tried to dry out some of my stuff. The tent leaks quite a bit so that it is impossible to keep things from getting damp.

For lunch, we had a fish chowder made with five grayling; an excellent dish! About 2:00 the rain stopped, but the sky looked threatening, so we decided to stay put for the rest of the day. Everyone disappeared to get food. Joe gathered blueberries and mushrooms: a small white kind with smooth skins. They are quite good fried and took the place of starch at dinner. Bruce caught a lot of lake trout, and I shot three ptarmigan in a spruce grove back in the bush. They are hard to get a shot at because they fly up, land and then creep around and hide under bushes, so that you can't see where they are unless you crawl in after them.

Caribou are all over the place. They are constantly looking at us from a ridge just across the river from camp. A party of two could live off the country without caribou, but by shooting caribou as you went, you could really supply any number.

No new decision has been reached on the rapid question, except that I proposed that we paddle across the river up here, line the canoes down the left shore to the eddy and portage from there, if the eddy is impossible to get to any other way. This is probably what we will do.

Skip | AUGUST 18, DUBAWNT RIVER

We have been camped here at this rapid for so long now that it has been affectionately dubbed "Son of a Bitch!"

Art and I spent the morning scouting the w shore after a tricky crossing and returned with the dilemma still unresolved. The eddies which would lead to a portage point seem extremely dangerous and rocky, and are bordered by very swift current; the rapid itself is unknown. However, during lunch and motivated as much by exasperation and the desire to move "almost anywhere," we decided to try shooting the rapid with a half-loaded canoe; sent the four others off with the remainder of the canoe load and prepared for our attempt. But in the meantime, heavy winds drove in a rain squall, preventing us from moving.

So we spent the rest of a cold, disappointing day huddled in the tent speaking in cautious terms of food vs. time, and comforting ourselves somewhat by recollections of other expeditions and the ability of men to prevail under many trying circumstances . . . we ignore the disasters.

Sunshine momentarily again and dinner is being prepared.

After a store-bought meal of glop and cocoa, Art and I will attempt to shoot the rapid; later entry will tell the story . . . rain continued intermittently after dinner and so we retired to the tents anticipating an early and exciting day tomorrow, weather permitting.

Grilled a ptarmigan on a green spit after dinner and was delighted with the taste, wild, almost salty.

Skip | AUGUST 19, DUBAWNT RIVER

AM. Well, we finally shot and the beauty and the pride and confidence of overcoming a difficult obstacle pervades us all. After breakfast, Art and I took the half-loaded canoe and pushed off 'midst "good lucks" and many personal butterflies. Once we got going everything went according to plan and three fleeting miles later we stopped in a small eddy, exhausted from both exertion and tension.

The first is always the worst and by the time I had gone back to take the second canoe through the rapid, it had already become old stuff. I am sitting on our red food box now below the rapid waiting for Pete to bring the last canoe down. Lunch will follow and then we will pack up and leave this most troublesome obstruction, moving on to the next.

PM. The rest of the afternoon was spent in an exhilarating ride down the swift, sharply defined river as it flowed thru beautiful bedrock canyons in long sweeping S turns. After the last few days of hesitation and inactivity, the sense of pushing rapidly and easily northward is wonderful. As we sped along, the caribou ranged the cliffs and ridges at the river's bank, and often, as a large buck stood motionless against the skyline, I had the feeling that this must have been the Indians plight years ago; to stand motionless and watch as strangers silently invaded the country. Today this country seems to belong to the caribou and we are the strangers.

We are camped at what Tyrrell named, "half-way hill" from which he is supposed to have seen Dubawnt Lake for the first time. After dinner we will re-enact this little episode in the hope that the lake is still there. (Wrong Hill!)

Peter | AUGUST 19, DUBAWNT RIVER

After breakfast, Art and Skip were ready to try again. I walked down to the cliff and watched. The current swept them a little wide around the first bend and the lightened canoe was bouncing all over the place as it hit some big waves, but they made it into the right shore all right, then shot the water going past the cliff on the right, just between the boulders and the big waves. They pulled over at the tail. Then Skip and I went back and I came down in the bow of his canoe. The waves look too much for a canoe with our present loads, but by taking out only two food packs, our canoe was light enough to get down without shipping water. Bruce went back with me and came down in the bow of my canoe, I in the stern.

We had lunch then, out from under the shadow of that obstacle at last, then started down the river again. This stretch is very beautiful, swift current going down between narrow banks with no serious rapids. We came through a small lake and a few wide places in the river. In one, the river spread out and shallowed considerably, so there was some danger of running into rocks. The country changes; the sides of the river are rocky cliffs now. This country is so varied that you can't keep up with the changes, they come so fast.

We camped after making about 15 mi. on the south end of a fairly long lake. The hills are growing flatter as we approach Dubawnt Lake. All today we have been seeing scattered spruce groves and we are near one now. It is hard to believe that we will be running out of wood entirely so soon.

Skip | AUGUST 20, "HALF WAY HILL"

Wind and a serious need for meat dictate a day in camp. While Art and Bruce went hunting with camera and gun respectively, I took the .22 and spent the morning chasing ptarmigan . . . box score one dead bird . . . the Great White Hunter! Covered a lot of territory however and saw the characteristic rings of stone and crude rock statue which designate Eskimo territory for the first time. This region probably marks the limit of their SW wandering.

Butchering and hanging the meat took most of the afternoon, and then into early evening was devoted to initial scraping of a new hide. This is a difficult and tedious job, but although the hide has a few holes in it and some of the winter hair, it will be a welcome /smelly blanket in the cold weather to come. It hangs stretching to dry overnight and then the scraping continues.

Turned cold tonight, dropping to 38F at sundown. A hot Detroit summer seems a long way off.

Peter | AUGUST 20, "HALF WAY HILL"

Very cold and windy this morning, so Art decided to declare a day of rest and kill a caribou. He and Bruce went out to kill one from the canoe. Skip took the .22 and went after ptarmigan. I took a long walk to pick blueberries and see how many ptarmigan I could flush. I saw quite a few easy shots that morning. Joe picked mushrooms and got a good pot full for dinner. The best kind are rounded and brown on top with a spongy underside.

After hunting all morning, Skip came back with only one ptarmigan. I thought this was ridiculous, so I went out and hunted all afternoon, and only killed one. I saw a great many, but not until they flew up. Then they wouldn't come down for quite a while and I couldn't get a shot at them.

When I got back to camp, I found the caribou already butchered and hung with Skip working on the hide. Bruce and Art had no trouble finding one close to the shore. Then they just loaded him in the canoe and headed back to camp.

Tyrrell

[F]rom the crest of a low hill near the last grove of small black spruce, we saw before us a great lake apparently covered with a solid sheet of ice. Our journey by water seemed to be at an end, and the men were anxious to turn back; but we pushed on and when we reached the lake we found a narrow lane of open water close to the shore on which we could travel with our canoes between the ice and the land.

We shall have to be living more and more off the country in the future. We have only eight meals of macaroni left and about twenty-five half-pound packages of potatoes. This is our entire supply of starch.

It has been quite cold the last two days. The meat should keep much better than it did the last time.

Skip | AUGUST 21, DUBAWNT LAKE

The "great lake" day has finally arrived!

After paddling most of the day against a cold, gusty headwind, we reached the shore of this tremendous lake. And although we are still among the river islands, the occasional glimpse between the smaller islands affords an impressive view of this immense body of water. It resembles any of the Great Lakes in coastal view and certainly is awe-inspiring when we contemplate crossing it by canoe. The lake extends north for 60 miles and we expect to cover almost 100 in coastline travel. As yet there is no sign of ice and in spite of near freezing weather, I will be quite surprised to see any ice pack; the sun seems too prevalent.

Our main concern is fair weather for the next few days. The wind has been the most serious handicap and has almost become characteristic of a day in the North. Rain is not a serious threat although unpleasant enough at times.

The camp was bothered by wolves for the first time tonight. Four of a larger pack (we could hear the howling) appeared on a ridge by camp and one was bold enough to come very close to a tent. We have a large quantity of meat hanging about which must be quite a tempting item for these powerful animals. As yet our curiosity and inexperience displaces any fear of attack.

The thermometer was broken today, so from now on temperatures will only be impressions, until the water freezes.

Peter | AUGUST 21, DUBAWNT LAKE

Fairly easy, though cold, trip down to Dubawnt Lake. The country has flattened out considerably and has grown quite barren of trees. Not a single stick of wood in sight from the top of a hill. There is still grass and caribou everywhere though. I won't feel completely exposed to the elements and naked in the wilderness until they are gone. Somehow, the caribou are a great blessing and a softening of the land. It is its one source of plenty. We still managed to pick up enough driftwood for a cook fire tonight.

Skip | AUGUST 22, DUBAWNT LAKE

Storm-bound on Dubawnt Lake.

We left camp this morning battling an increasing W wind and within 2 hr., the breeze had veered to the NW and built up such a sea that we were forced to pull in at the first favorable spot.

Tyrrell

Shortly after entering the lake we were delayed for three days by a heavy storm of wind and cold rain, which afterwards turned to snow; and . . . as we were leaving camp, there was a thin skin of ice on the tarpaulins.

Used the primus stove for the first time today. The trees have long since left us and we now seem to be on the northern fringe of the driftwood. Campsites must now be chosen primarily to afford shelter from the almost inevitable wind. Steep cliffs and abrupt hills with S or E exposure are now looked upon with the same gleeful eye that a small grove of spruce received a week or so ago.

One definite advantage of the "cold camp" is that we all will get more sleep. With no fire to warm us and that magnetic pot of tea, we retire to our tents soon after eating. We can only afford to use the stove quickly for a meal and then the sputtering flame is turned off by a reluctant hand.

The country has once again changed its appearance as we travel north. With the last of the trees nestled in the shallow valleys, we left the exposed bedrock ridges and higher hills. The land retains its ridge appearance on a smaller scale now and is covered with varying sized boulders, some tremendous size, all generally covered with gray-green lichens and laying among low ground cover and pebbles. Tall grasses still exist in the hollows, but the characteristic cover has become lichen, moss, bear berry and arctic birch.

Peter | AUGUST 22, DUBAWNT LAKE

Blowing hard today. We made 4 mi. in the morning, then had to hole up for protection from the north wind. We are still flushing lots of ptarmigan but they are still almost impossible to get a shot at.

I was not feeling too well today, probably from eating too much caribou yesterday, and sat around scraping my caribou hide all afternoon. At the rate we are going, I will have to have a complete winter outfit before long.

If we do get held up on Dubawnt Lake for very long, our situation certainly seems serious. We are out of danger as long as we can find caribou, but if they are gone, we have had it, unless we get a lot of good traveling weather, which doesn't seem likely in this neck of the woods. The change in weather and in the whole atmosphere and mood of the country is so sudden it is like a blow. On the river we were much more protected. Here the country is exposed to all the effects of the weather.

Skip | AUGUST 23, DUBAWNT LAKE

There is a limit beyond which knowledge of grim circumstances need not be confided to the crew. This does not mean that the men should not be aware of a situation, but rather that a general statement of the condition is enough. The details and possibilities of future discomfort should be kept quiet and whenever possible any announcement of short rations or other additional hardship should be accompanied by some sort of positive plan of action to combat the discomfort.

This morning Art entertained us with the account of Tyrrell's grim trip from here to Baker Lake and seemed obsessed with relating all sorts of futures for the group. This did nothing more than make people all the more conscious of our predicament with very little encouragement.

No action was taken until finally a slight squall chased us to our tents where we stayed until 3 PM. In the meantime, the wind veered directly out of the N, sending the temperature down abruptly and clearing the sky. We left camp at 4:30 PM in the face of this very cold N wind and after sneaking from one lee to another for a few miles we were again forced to make camp due to the mounting seas and wind.

Our feet and hands are continually cold and to get either wet has become a serious accident. Travel conditions have changed completely since the southern forest days when we were forever stepping in and out of the water without much thought.

Our total mileage for the last few days amounts to about six miles and so it seems that Dubawnt Lake with a helping hand from the weatherman is doing her best to keep us pinned against her southern shore. With about 25 days left, we have had to cut almost our entire food consumption in ½. We still have plenty of meat, but the lack of fat and starches make dinner rather unsatisfying. At home the cuts and quantities of meat we consume would be unbelievable in terms of price and availability. A good size caribou lasts about 4 days. One hind quarter per meal, both roast strips for one meal, and two front quarters for another meal. The miscellaneous cuts go for breakfast and lunch extras.

Am now in the midst of scraping down my caribou hide and find the job rather laborious although it is fun to repeat the native process with stone scraper and brain. The hide is very useful now, serving as a sleeping pad at night to insulate the floor of the tent and as a lap robe while paddling during the day.

After dinner this evening, which has become a cold meal since the cold weather set in; the plates and food cooling off almost instantly, only hot item is the tea; we have once again decided on emergency scheduling and will get up at 4 AM if the wind is down, paddle until 8 or so, have breakfast and continue paddling until the wind stops us again. It is interesting to note that these measures initially come from one of the gang, seldom from Art. In any case, I am confident we will arrive at Baker in good time and with plenty of meat on our bones.

Skip | AUGUST 24, DUBAWNT LAKE

Heavy frost and a frozen milk pail greeted us this morning as we shivered out of the sack at 4 AM; hurriedly gulped down hardtack and jam, and set off in a frosted canoe hoping to make a few miles at least before the wind came up. As luck would have it, the day remained absolutely calm and we were able to continue paddling the entire day with a break around 9 AM for breakfast and another at 2 PM for lunch.

Now at 6 PM we have made camp and are very happy with the day's run. Just before we stopped, Art threw out his line and soon hauled in a 12-lb. lake trout which is boiling now for a chowder dinner. Lake trout have been quite easy to catch ever since we hit the river. They are near the surface and readily take a Dare Devil so we have enjoyed fish for breakfast most every day and every 3 days or so a fish dinner. Meat certainly is no problem.

We are now better than ⅓ of the way through the lake and spirits rise . . . supplies at present consumption should see us through. Big worry now is the cold. We all are wearing 3 or 4 layers of clothing and only the occasional sun or vigorous exercise warms us . . . another few weeks may bring serious trouble. But for the present it merely serves to keep us damn busy.

Peter | AUGUST 24, DUBAWNT LAKE

George woke us at 4:30 this morning. The lake was quite calm at last, but cold. There was a thick coating of frost everywhere and it was impossible to keep warm unless you were very active. We bolted down a hardtack and loaded up in a hurry.

We made Teall Point in about three hours and cooked breakfast there on the end of the point. There is not a scrap of driftwood anywhere now, so we have to use the gas stove. Oats sure tasted good after a 6 mi. paddle in the cold.

After breakfast, we started paddling again and made it quite a ways, past Snow Island, a point on the northwest shore, where we had lunch. While we were resting before we got to the point, Art dragged the Dare Devil for about one minute and caught a 12-lb. lake trout. For such a barren looking lake, the Dubawnt must be swarming with fish.

After lunch, we kept going for another four hours, but an east wind sprang up, so we headed for the west side of a long island that had a deep narrow bay marked in it on the map. We made this about 6:00, feeling pretty tired, but pleased with ourselves after a long day. In a straight line from parallel to parallel, we made 23 mi., but we must have paddled closer to thirty.

Dubawnt Lake no longer seems so threatening and much more beautiful now. On the northwest shore, there are some beautiful mountains, not especially high, but mountains in this country. They are flat on top like big mesas out west. If I ever make this trip again, I would sure like to do some exploring in these hills. The country is all so open that you could walk anywhere. The only obstacles are streams and rivers that would have to be crossed.

This narrow bay is a beautiful camp site. I walked down north along the shore and caught an 8-lb. lake trout before dinner on Art's casting rig. They don't put up much of a fight for their size, but I had a few exciting moments before I landed him.

We have found that the low, green cover that looks like heath will burn. It makes a quick hot fire for boiling things, but leaves no embers for frying. Still it is easy to gather a large pile of the stuff and it is fine for warming yourself or drying clothes. This discovery makes me feel a lot better and not so afraid of freezing with insufficient clothes. I can always go off and build my own heather fire to keep warm. A party of two could do all their cooking by this stuff, though it wouldn't be very convenient.

Skip | AUGUST 25, "PITCAIRN" ISLAND

Today was certainly the most beautiful of the summer. We spent the day camped in a tiny landlocked inlet on this softly rolling, grassy, pebble-beached, rocky-cliffed retreat which reminds me of precisely what Nordoff & Hall must have had in mind as their haven for the mutineers. From the meadow above the wave-pounded cliffs the deep blue water of the lake stretches on for sparkling miles. The sun shimmers on the water like a summer full moon and wispy white clouds dance across the pale blue sky. I walked from our sheltered camp through soft moist meadows filled with brilliant patches of Arctic cotton to the steep shore at the N end of the island and sat a top a large rock looking out to "sea."

Dreams, plans, awe contentedly flood my being and over it all, the strengthening conviction that to deny these moments of exhilaration and significance from my means of livelihood would wither too much of what has become my soul. Perhaps 100 yrs. too late; perhaps doomed to a mediocre life of impracticality; but in any case a whole, complete person. The service takes up the next two years. And then perhaps geology as a means to land in the West . . . this need not be Failure!

After dinner, another flare up; this time Art boyishly insisting that we have hot tea and finally, a complete breakfast before starting off at 4:30 AM mornings. At times we all seem to be too small for our jobs.

Skip | AUGUST 26, DUBAWNT LAKE

Left camp at 5 AM after breakfast and were met almost immediately by large, ocean-like rollers running the length of the lake and pounding against the weather shore of our tiny island. We were able to duck in behind another chain of islands for a few more miles. Midmorning brunch break was rather exciting; covey of four ptarmigan killed with a hunting knife. And the grand booby prize of the trip to Pessl for swamping his canoe while standing up to put on a parka. Damn near tipped the whole works over. Cold hour spent drying slightly damp hardtack and very wet Skip after having to dive for dishes in about four feet of icy water. Warm sun soon took care of both and we were off again, stopping within an hour due to high winds and a nearby herd of caribou.

Made camp on a grassy slope of a large island SW of Outlet Bay; bagged a caribou and enjoyed ptarmigan stew for dinner.

Have generally adopted early morning departure, so early to bed.

Peter | AUGUST 26, DUBAWNT LAKE

While Skip was standing up taking a piss out of the canoe, he slipped and fell on the gunnel and the whole works almost went over. He got all wet and the canoe partly filled, but we soon got ashore and dried everything. We couldn't find any heather for a fire, but the dwarf birch works and that's everywhere.

While we were coasting in the lee of a large island, we spotted a caribou and Joe got out to kill it, but missed with his 30/30. We decided to camp here anyway, as the wind was too strong to travel. Bruce went out after lunch and killed a caribou conveniently close to the water where we could paddle right up and load him in the canoe.

I went for a walk that afternoon and just reveled in the beauty of these barren grounds with the sun on them. The golden grass and the deep blue of the lake make a lovely picture. Dubawnt Lake is becoming an idyllic place now.

Skip | AUGUST 27, DUBAWNT LAKE

Questionable winds and general early morning reluctance combined to form another beautiful day in camp.

Art was occupied with stretching his caribou skin and once again showed his rather annoying tendency to pass off personal preferences as group decisions; however, these things are minor, probably not even noticeable to one who had not built such an inspiration around one man.

By now I have placed myself beyond the group haggles and enjoy an easy feeling of "come what may," which certainly eases most of my tensions but often leaves me with the role of arbitrator.

In the late afternoon Pete, Art and I paddled to the main land and spent about 3 hrs. roaming among the rather rare high ridges of this region. Game was abundant. Everywhere I looked caribou were moving about, birds were chattering and fluttering continually and I saw my first arctic fox with a shimmering blue-gray coat. Many sandhill cranes can be seen and overall the rich red & yellow of frost-nipped ground cover lent a beautiful reminder of the oncoming winter.

From the ridges, this immense country stretches on seemingly into the infinite. The grazing animals, endless plains and misty, unbroken horizon create an overwhelming surge of insignificance for this lone man wandering in strangeness and natural neutrality. Mankind seems to find its proper place again as merely one of the kingdom, and the false values of a hurried, blinded society easily fall away. The furious race for wealth and position seem ridiculous here and the contentment of simplicity certainly worth the sacrifice of an extra station wagon.

Peter | AUGUST 27, DUBAWNT LAKE

Another good day, but still a breeze from the south. We could have traveled, but Art declared a day of rest because he wanted to go over to the mainland and see what it is like; what animals he could get pictures of. Skip and I went with him.

I accepted the dictum of a day of rest with some reluctance. I am the only member of the party anxious to get to Baker Lake as soon as possible. The feeling is compounded of several causes; the biggest is that I would very much like to get to Harvard on time. I don't know why this should be. I don't like the place that much. Other factors are that I don't have enough warm clothes and no protection from the rain. Also, I want to get enough food as soon as I can. But the country is so beautiful now, it would be a shame to hurry through it.

Actually today turned out to be somewhat cloudy and not up to the high standards of the other days we have been having lately, but the

Tyrrell

[W]e found the outlet of the lake, having followed the shore for 117 miles.

mainland was still fascinating. For some reason, it has been nipped by the frost more than the island, so the autumn colors are much more pronounced. The dwarf birch varies from a pale yellow to a deep russet and the smaller ground cover plant is bright crimson. The grass is darker yellow with a little orange in it, but on a dark day like this one, these colors play a minor part and the dominant theme is a brownish-gray of rolling hills stretching off into the distance.

We saw a lot of caribou. After lunch, we split up and I, after walking off for quite a ways, sat down behind some rocks to rest. After a bit, I looked up and saw a small calf not ten feet from me. Peeking over the rocks, I saw two does and a fine buck join it. I could have killed any one of them with a .22 or even a spear. The wind was blowing toward me and they couldn't get my scent and slowly grazed right past.

Later that afternoon, I saw an Arctic fox at about twenty feet. We stood and stared at each other for quite a while. Then he gave a little snort and bounded off, looking at me over his shoulder. Arctic ground squirrels were thick everywhere. They are just like prairie dogs. They sit up by their holes and stare at you and then dive down with a little cry of warning.

When we got back to camp, we found Bruce with two big fish, 6 and 8 lb.

This afternoon on the mainland, I saw my first wolf. The open country gives one a peculiar feeling when you see so much going on. It is like the ants nest with glass sides. We could see the wolf stalking the caribou and the caribou nervously keeping its distance. I am used to having things hidden by the woods. It seems strange to stand on a hill and watch it all.

This caribou had more fat on him than the others and we could peel enough off the neck and shoulders to fry the meat without bacon. I never

Members of the 1955 Moffatt Dubawnt party ready for transport from Stony Rapids to the put-in at Black Lake. From the left, back row: Bruce LeFavour, Peter Franck, Art Moffatt; front row: George Grinnell, Skip Pessl, Joe Lanouette. Courtesy of Creigh Moffatt.

Black Lake put-in; food and gear stockpiled on the beach, ready to load; wildfire smoke in the distance. Courtesy of Creigh Moffatt.

Typical muskeg vegetation: spruce, birch, alder, willow, water lily, and grasses along the Chipman (Wolverine) portage at the northwest corner of Black Lake. Courtesy of Creigh Moffatt.

George Grinnell adjusts the tumpline on one of the kitchen boxes. Courtesy of Creigh Moffatt.

Quiet water and marshy shorelines approaching the height-of-land. Courtesy of Creigh Moffatt.

Approaching the steep, rocky terrain of a moraine ridge along a Chipman River portage toward Bompas Lake. Courtesy of Creigh Moffatt.

Wildfire burning in spruce/birch stand along an esker-ridge crest, Wholdaia Lake. Courtesy of Creigh Moffatt.

Wind-bound on Wholdaia Lake; temperature 40F, July 24. Courtesy of Creigh Moffatt.

Windy campsite amid stunted spruce and lichen-covered bedrock. World War II Army surplus two-man mountain tents, reinforced with a canvas rain fly, offered sanctuary from nasty weather and voracious bugs. Courtesy of Creigh Moffatt.

Gloomy camp on Boyd Lake; monotonous wind-blown drizzle and 40F. Courtesy of Creigh Moffatt.

After a squall on Boyd Lake; caribou parts wind-drying on a tripod rack. Courtesy of Creigh Moffatt.

“Tumping the Beast.” Art Moffatt carrying the camera/film box on a tumpline. The box weighed nearly eighty pounds and was one of the few loads that did not get lighter as we traveled. Courtesy of Creigh Moffatt.

Dubawnt River south of Markham Lake; high rocky hills confine the winding river in broad sweeping curves; rare, isolated stunted spruce occupy some tributary drainages. Courtesy of Creigh Moffatt.

Lichen-covered boulders dominate the landscape in the vicinity of Barlow Lake. Small lakes bordered by muskeg and occasional small stands of stunted spruce and larch interrupt the gently undulating boulder fields. Courtesy of Creigh Moffatt.

Hunter's cabin on the Dubawnt River south of Markham Lake. Courtesy of Creigh Moffatt.

Nicholson Lake; caribou common but in small groups of three to ten; trees are thinning out but still plenty of wood for cook fires. Courtesy of Creigh Moffatt.

Skip Pessl using a stone scraper to soften a caribou hide which then was used as a lap robe while canoeing and as a sleeping pad at night. Courtesy of Creigh Moffatt.

Idyllic camp in a small, protected bay on the northwest shore of Dubawnt Lake. Skip carries dried heather and willow twigs to camp for the evening cook fire. Courtesy of Creigh Moffatt.

Art at camp on the shore of Dubawnt Lake, stretching a fresh caribou hide and scraping off any residual flesh. Courtesy of Creigh Moffatt.

“Shirts Off” afternoon on Dubawnt Lake, August 30.
Courtesy of Creigh Moffatt.

Skip and Bruce finish building a cairn on a prominent bedrock hill overlooking Outlet Bay at the northeast end of Dubawnt Lake. "Arrow" rock points northeasterly toward the outlet gorge flowing into Grant Lake. Courtesy of Creigh Moffatt.

Heavy rapids on Dubawnt River below Dubawnt Lake, approaching the powerful gorge draining to Grant Lake. Courtesy of Creigh Moffatt.

Wind swept, snow-bound island cache at the south end of Marjorie Lake; camera/film box in foreground, canoe sheltering Art Moffatt's body middle ground. RCMP reconnaissance flight located cache and recovered the body in November 1955. Photo credit Clair Dent, RCMP Officer, Baker Lake, Nunavut, Canada, courtesy of Creigh Moffat.

Burial of Art Moffatt, 1919–1955, at the community cemetery, Baker Lake, Nunavut, Canada. Photo credit Clair Dent, RCMP Officer, Baker Lake, Nunavut, Canada, courtesy of Creigh Moffatt.

seem to grow tired of caribou as I think I would of beef. It has certainly improved our diet and saved us from feeling awfully hungry on a lot of nights.

Skip | AUGUST 28, OUTLET BAY

AM. The last few days have been a delightful succession of sun, blue sky and warmth. The gentle rumble of rolling waves breaking on sandy beaches and rocky cliffs has constantly been in the air as background music to this leisurely time of hiking, hunting and extremely peaceful living.

A fine breakfast of oats, caribou liver, lake trout roe and tea sent us on an open water journey across two big bays of the lake. The waves were rolling large, but soft, in the gentle breeze, and the clear sky and bright sun created a brilliant setting of deep water and shimmering waves.

The wind freshened at noon and we pulled in to the lee of a large grassy island, where we will have lunch and wait for the wind to lessen.

As the water for fish chowder heats on the beach, off on a rocky point, the .22 cracks frequently as George does his best to provide us another ptarmigan dinner.

During the leisurely paddle this morning, I thought about the prospects of a career in forestry. It seems that there would be many aspects of the industry to survey and it might hold the key to my quest for a means of livelihood without the sacrifice of a way of life in nature and wilderness.

PM. We paddled continuously until 9 PM and reached the middle portion of Outlet Bay. Our camp is at the foot of a sizeable hill, which should provide a fine view if the morning is clear, and if the present darkness has not exaggerated too much.

We have now spent a week on this lake and have experienced north and south winds, both with W & E variations and have seen no sign of ice whatsoever. Ever since passing Tyrrell's cairn at the south lake entrance, we have been expecting some sort of ice pack to appear on the horizon. But the conditions have been to the contrary; warm, sunny days defy any iceberg. I think this is indicative of more than a seasonal variation. Throughout Tyrrell's journal he speaks of seeing patches of snow well to the south and he suffered his first snow storm on August 10. We are fortunate to enjoy the warm change, even if it diminishes a bit of the romantic challenge of the trip.

Peter | AUGUST 28, OUTLET BAY

We got off to a pretty late start today. Art was scraping his hide long after the rest of us were packed up and ready to go. It is a clear, fine day, still with the due south breeze. The waves on the open lake were big rollers again as we set off away from the land, heading east out toward a large island. We paddled for two hours without stopping and made it to this large island for lunch. There I climbed to the top and looked around for landmarks as we still didn't know where we were. I got a beautiful view from here. I could see Outlet Bay far off in the distance and could pretty well tell where we were.

The deep blue of the water contrasting with the tawny hills made one of the most beautiful sights I have ever seen. While I was walking up the hill, I saw a few sitting ptarmigan, easy shots. When I walked closer, a flock of nine got up. By the time that I got to the bottom of the hill, George had killed seven. Apparently, the whole island is full of them.

We had a fish chowder for lunch using 15 lb. of fish Bruce had caught the day before and were so full we could hardly move. We have been living like kings off the land here. There is surely no danger of starvation as long as we can fish and hunt.

After an hour's rest, we shoved off again, going east so as to get a favorable wind down the second island to the bay, the one on the east side. Art delayed for more pictures and then wasn't sure about the way, but we made it 10 mi. further to a deep narrow bay behind a high hill, quite conspicuous from the water on the left side. By the time that we finally camped, it was dark. We tried the ptarmigan in the glop, just boiled, and they were delicious; better than broiled.

Skip | AUGUST 29, OUTLET BAY

The leisurely breakfast of another "day off" saw us on our way to the top of the prominent hill overlooking our camp. And although it can only be

100–200 ft. high, it does afford a fine view and gives us some idea of the country to the north through which we will pass in a day or so.

The topography has changed once again from the ruddy conglomerate of a few miles south, to heavily bouldered granite gneiss piled high and sloping helter-skelter to the shore. Most of the boulders are covered with green, black and orange lichen, forming a desolate, but colorful, landscape. In the distance the land looks uniformly brown and forms a striking contrast with the rich blue water, which seems forever intent on gobbling up the entire landmass in its endless arms and bays.

We built a pretty big cairn a top the hill. Left a note inside and then spent the rest of the day wandering along the shore and nearby ridges.

Caught a few "lakers" for tomorrow's breakfast and enjoyed a good portion of fried roe for lunch. We are able to cook small portions of food over very smoky, smoldering fires by using dried grasses for tinder, piling on dead bits of heather, and then stoking continually with green dwarf-birch twigs. The process is troublesome, but certainly worth a hot noonday meal.

The sun dips low in the West now as I sit on a sunny rock point and look south into the vastness through which we have traveled. Home is somewhere in that vastness, and memories, expectations of my future linger in my mind. Yet it is with much reluctance that I realize within 15–20 days this most fascinating experience will be a distant, lasting memory. As time goes on, these next few weeks become more and more precious and are filled with ever increasing activity so as to glean as much as possible from this land of wonder and fascination.

Peter | AUGUST 29, OUTLET BAY

Windy this morning, so we stayed put. We made about 25 mi. the day before and are within 15 mi. of the mouth of the river, so everyone is feeling pretty pleased with themselves and the panic is off for a few days.

We all, except George, climbed a hill and built a cairn on top with a note inside. Then I took my lunch and set out for a walk cross country. It is a lovely country to walk on. Dry, hard clay underfoot with dwarf birch scarce enough so that they don't get in one's way. I had just gotten beyond the next range of hills when I saw a heavy thunder shower was bearing down in the distance, so I turned back. I found a line of stone men, quite obviously man made. They must have been raised by the Eskimos, but I can't imagine for what purpose. They couldn't have been used for driving caribou because they were in a valley and too close together.

I got back to camp about 4:00 and was so hungry I succumbed to the temptation to eat my entire supply of extra food I had saved up. They were only a drop in the bucket.

Bruce and I had a long chat. It seems he is not anxious to get back to college because he has lost his knack for creative writing, which is his best subject, so he wants to take the year off and travel through Europe or maybe join the Army. I haven't written a thing since the poem and story I wrote in sixth form year at St. Paul's; just haven't felt urge or have been too lazy when it came.

Bruce and I cut up the caribou meat and cooked dinner for Art as he was still out with his camera. I did the butchering, pulling the muscles of the hind legs as they came instead of cutting them off. It is quite a trick, but you get much better cuts that way.

A very pleasant, warm sunny day, but I would still like to see us do more traveling. I don't want to be any later to college than I have to.

Skip | AUGUST 30, DUBAWNT RIVER

Heavy winds and rain squalls chased us back into the tents this morning just as we were finishing our second cup of coffee, and a good thing it was, for I had prepared such a huge breakfast that none of us could have moved much farther than the tents anyway. I felt as if I would have crashed right through the bottom of the canoe and sunk like a stone if we would have been loading.

Inside the tent, half-way inside the sleeping bag, caribou hide around my shoulders, pipe lit, I listened in a contented stupor to the storm outside. Warm, full and delightfully secure, it was one of those rare times when the tiny tent seems as spacious and impenetrable as a stone castle.

After a brief snooze to regain at least some of my food-chased senses,

I finished reading Willis' book, *Across the Top of the World.* Names such as Misstaka, Takla Makass, Baltit, Nanga Parbat, Karakorum, Kaskin, Haindaz all hold suggestions of the completely new; things wonderful, things horrible. To think that over half the people in the world and more than half the land are completely foreign to me, not only in terms of experience, but even in imagination. All told Willis spent one night and 2 days on foot crossing Misstaka Pass, and although his back injury and treatment throughout Sinkiang were painful and discomforting, the trip itself was made almost entirely by train, auto and horse, and his periods of deprivation were always offset by intervals of lavish hospitality . . . not too bad!

After lunch, skies cleared and we enjoyed one more rare "shirts off" day as we paddled the remaining 15 miles across the bay to the outlet of the lake; warm, slight breezes . . . exhilarating; and as we approached the narrowing, we gradually became conscious of the increasing current while in the distance the almost forgotten river sounds of rushing water and rumbling rapids gradually became audible.

We are back on the river now, floating on a current strengthened by the entire drainage of the huge lake and driving toward the long, treacherous 2½-mile outlet rapid flowing through a steep canyon and finally settling in Grant Lake.

Peter | AUGUST 30, DUBAWNT RIVER

Raining when I woke up, but we had breakfast just the same, a heavy one with lots of fish and roe. We are getting low on gas now. Skip thinks we have enough for less than a week at our present rate of consumption.

After breakfast, I borrowed Shaw's "Man and Superman" from Skip and read through that in the tent all morning. I find him very entertaining and witty with his cynical Irish wit, but somehow rather meaningless with no depth to what he says.

By lunch, things had begun to clear up some and we finally got off about 4:00 in sunlight, heading for the mouth of the river. We took our time, catching fish on the way, and got to the mouth of the river in lovely clear weather about 7:00. For the first time in many weeks, we were troubled with black flies when we landed, but these soon stopped when the sun went down.

I think part of the reason I am so anxious to get to Baker Lake is because I am tired of being in a group so long. I want to do things my own way, when and how I please, instead of having to wait or hurry up for everyone else. I have been thinking of my walking trips in the Sierras recently as a lot of fun. I was lonely, but I was my own master and I did my traveling and cooking on my own without feeling dependent upon someone else. I guess this desire to do things alone is a natural product of being in the same bunch for so long, but I would like to do some camping alone again soon, particularly the cooking.

Skip | AUGUST 31, DUBAWNT RIVER

Beautiful morning of sun and successful rapid shooting gave us high hopes that we would be camped this evening at the beginning of the long portage to Grant Lake. Two long rapids before lunch and a long difficult one after were negotiated with little trouble and we then pulled up in a bay to scout the approach to the gorge.

I spent about 3 hours walking along the river, sketching routes through the remaining rapids and finally reached a high bluff where the portage follows the rim of the gorge. I was walking alone, sun was hot, a gentle breeze blowing, and I gazed down into the foaming pool below. Here I was, standing on a spot where few, if any, white men had ever been. How many would ever experience the cascading beauty of this scene; the rocky barrens as the background, with scattered caribou roaming slowly southward; dark shadows of large trout disturb the crystal clear reflections of the still waters, and the boiling surges of the roar beyond. Over my right shoulder the turquoise water of Grant Lake stretches as an enticing reward for the coming strenuous portage. Cortez, Balboa, Nansen, Drake all seemed within my grasp. Finally I broke the spell, took off my woolen shirt and long underwear for the hot return to the canoe, left them under a rock, and hurried back to the others.

When I reached them, the wind had shifted slightly and a strengthening

NW wind was blowing. Try as I may, I couldn't impress upon the rest the necessity to hurry; the mood of the early day was not to be broken so easily. And by the time we were on the river, the wind was very strong and gusty.

The first rapid was run under very difficult conditions due to the wind and its effect on the waves, and we were forced to make camp on the opposite (W) bank of the river in the lee of the approaching NW storm, just a few miles from my beauty spot and, incidentally, from my shirt and underwear. We were lucky to find some dry birch twigs on this bank however, and with 5 stoking and one cooking, were able to cook a meal without the use of our precious fuel supply.

It seems that we are continually faced with some shortage problem. Now that we have rationed our food supply sufficiently for the remainder of the trip, we are running out of gas. Estimate about 3 days supply left. Woe is me . . . raw meat is not too bad, but raw oats and macaroni may be too much!

The birch grows very twisted and low to the ground and generally has a few dead branches in each cluster. These are about the size of a pencil at the thickest. We collect them in bundles; break them into 6" sections and pile them under and around the sides of the pot . . . then the chore begins, to keep ahead of the flame and not run out of sticks. Oh for a good solid pine log!

Peter | AUGUST 31, DUBAWNT RIVER

Still warm and sunny today. We got going down the river fairly early. I looked over the first rapid and then went ahead, while Skip stayed behind to wait for Art. I just got through the first rapid when I remembered I had forgotten my hide. It was too late, I thought, to go back and I was sure Art would see it anyway, so I kept on going through the next two. Then I stopped to look one over that went around a bend to the right. It looked easy to shoot on the right side, so I walked down to look at the next. I didn't really take a careful look, but what I did see looked easy, so I walked back to where I had left the canoe. By this time, Art and Skip had caught up. They got out to look at the first one, but took my word that the next was easy, so I jumped in the canoe and shot down first. Either I got too far to the left or I had underestimated the power of the rapid, or both. Anyway, we hit some awfully big waves and took in more than an inch of water. I pulled over to dump and Skip pulled over to look at the next one I had said was easy. It turned out that the waves were much bigger and more powerful than I had thought. We decided to wait for Art and then run it close to the right shore, just missing a big wave on the right coming out from the shore.

While we were walking back from looking at the rapids, Skip saw a gray wolf on the far side of the river, running upstream. Apparently, Art saw it too because he stayed put and took pictures. By this time, I was getting rather worried about my hide as Art said he hadn't seen it. I was on the point of walking back 4 mi. when Art came around the bend and finally produced it, saying, "Let this be a lesson, etc." Feeling much relieved, I enjoyed lunch.

Then Skip shot through the first rapid with Art taking pictures by the big wave. Skip got through with a little water by going outside the wave with plenty of clearance. I thought I could do better than this, so I started out close to the shore, thinking the current would carry me out around the wave. Unfortunately, it did nothing of the kind and I hit the outside of the white breaker. A big sheet of water crashed down into the canoe. We took about two inches of water right there. I kept on going, but the canoe was awfully sluggish and there were a lot more waves ahead. I just hung on and tried to avoid the worst. Once we almost tipped over and more water kept sloping in. We finally made calm water and pulled up with about three inches of water in the bottom. Fortunately none of the supplies had gotten wet, only both our personal packs. George was a very surly boy when he pulled his stuff out and found his books soaking wet.

I left him to brood and climbed up on the bank to see if I could find the best spot to portage. I walked a long way and couldn't find much. Black flies were very bad. Skip came in later and said the best plan would be to go down the river, shoot the next two rapids and start the portage just above the gorge where the river becomes impassable for 2.5 mi. We went on down a lovely wide stretch of the river, one of the most beautiful spots in it that I have seen yet. The banks are about thirty feet high on both sides and drop steeply to the river, which flows swift and calm. It is like going through a great tunnel. Then the wind started to come up and was blowing hard in our faces when we got to the first rapid. We shot it all right on the left, but the wind made things very hard. The head of the portage was only a mile on past the second rapid, but we didn't want to try shooting the second rapid in this high wind, so we pulled over to the left bank (portage was on the right) for protection and made camp.

Landing was poor, but the spot we picked turned out to be an old Eskimo campsite with quite conspicuous and well-made tent rings of rocks piled in a perfect circle.

It looks like we are in for some bad weather tonight; a strong wind from the west blowing in heavy clouds.

Skip | SEPTEMBER 1, DUBAWNT RIVER

The twig marathon continued for breakfast, complicated somewhat by a driving rain joining the cold, windy day about one-half way through the preparations. It was a cold and miserable cook who crawled back into the tent after gulping a few spoonfuls of oats and quantities of hot tea. Stayed there until 3 PM when we had a bowl of soup for lunch.

Rain stopped and after running like crazy through the boulders and grass to get warm, I caught enough fish for a late dinner of chowder and tea. The caribou must think we are crazy, running like hell, arms waving and feet stomping with no particular direction in mind, just zig-zagging, to get the circulation going again. Times like this, I think they must be right in heading south.

As I look out the tent to windward, there seems to be a light streak far on the horizon; perhaps tomorrow will dawn clear and we will be able to reach the gorge at last, and maybe also a soggy shirt and underwear??

Skip | SEPTEMBER 2, DUBAWNT RIVER

Another bitch of a day, worse than yesterday by a long shot. Wind, rain, cold from dawn to darkness with very few intervals of relative calm. During one of those elusive moments about noon, I crawled out and began preparing our first meal of the day. Hot oats seemed appropriate. Building the tiny birch fire in a high wind with wet twigs just about ended the attempt, but finally got her going and the water heating when a terrific gale hit; driving rain and wind so hard that the canoes were lifted off the ground and sent tumbling down the rocky shore. At the very height of the storm, the pot somehow came to a boil and rather than give up, I sat there in the rain stirring a god damned pot of oats.

The rest were mustered out to secure the canoes and when that was finished, we all ate cold oats in the rain.

Back to the tents until a brief patch of sun drew us out like ground hogs late in the day. It remained clear until we were ready to eat our fish soup for dinner and then down it came again . . . "piss pot"!

September certainly is not very kind in its beginning; but the moon rose clear and full, so high expectations for tomorrow.

Peter | SEPTEMBER 2, DUBAWNT RIVER

Raining again and blowing hard this morning. The clouds are high and moving fast, but there seems to be no end to them, still quite cold. I couldn't keep warm sitting outside under the canoe, though my clothes are fairly dry. I am wearing everything I own now. I just put on my last sweater.

After lunch, things finally began to clear up and by 3:30 it was sunny and warm again, however there was still too much wind to move. Since we arrived at this spot, we have been using dwarf birch for firewood. It grows quite thick and tall here. It is a terrible nuisance to cook for six people on. You have to break off all the little twigs and just use the main stems and even then, you get a smoking fire that goes out unless it is tended constantly. However, it is better than nothing, so we are saving what little gas we have left for later on when we may not be able to find anything else to burn.

After it stopped raining, I did a little fishing and caught a nice trout in front of camp. We don't know what kind of fish these are. They look somewhat like the lake trout we have been catching, but there is a definite difference. The lake trout have much bigger heads with larger mouths.

The markings on the sides are in the same pattern, but the lake trout has white sides while these trout are dark all the way down to the belly and reddish there. They look pale golden when they are still alive and fighting in the water. The lake trout is not as heavily built or as deep bellied as these. They are longer and skinnier. These new fish we are calling Arctic char, though they might well be something else.

After I caught this fish, I walked down along the river to where it really narrows down and the impassable heavy rapids begin. It is impossible to describe the tremendous force and beauty of this long rapid. The channel narrows to about 25 yd. and enormous waves, 10 ft. high, shoot up. The whole river is a mass of white water rushing between the steep rock cliffs. The huge waves, building up and crashing down, have a hypnotic effect. One loses all sense of time and just stands looking in a daze.

When I did finally tear myself away, it was dinner time and more big thunderstorms were massing up to the south and west. On the way back, I noticed lots of driftwood along the shore. It must be branches that have broken off the dwarf trees at flood time in the Spring and then left along the banks.

This morning before breakfast, the wind was so strong that it picked up my canoe and blew it, rolling over and over, and bouncing high in the air, up the bank away from the river about 50 yd. I was so amazed, I just stood there for a bit. Then Bruce came running out and helped me put it back down in a hollow. This evening we talked about what we might do if all three canoes were blown into the river some night and lost. We figured we were only about 100 mi. as the crow flies from Baker Lake, with no other big rivers than the Dubawnt to cross, so we could theoretically walk out easily in ten days; but following the river, we have 200 mi. left as we swing westward before we start back east. Also, we still have 70 mi. north in a straight line to go before we get through.

Skip | SEPTEMBER 3, DUBAWNT RIVER

Another day of the same hellish weather, and after suffering through another breakfast, I crawled back into the tent and slept until 3 PM when soup was served for lunch.

Just couldn't go back to the tent, so bundled up, took an empty packsack and went on a long wood hunt. Felt like an old rag collector with my cotton-pickin' bag slung over my shoulder and eyes glued on the ground for any stray twig. Was quite successful with the twigs and, as is so often the case, found that once underway, a cold, rainy day is not nearly as bad as it looks from inside a tent.

Much to my surprise I saw my shirt and underwear on the other bank, so I hurried back to camp, got Bruce and we paddled to the other shore where I recovered my belongings.

While we were there, we walked down to the gorge and stood spellbound under the force of the mighty river fighting its way through the narrow rock passage. I have never experienced such an expression of power and unalterable force. Even in the gloom of this day, the white foam swirled in beautiful contrast to the dark rock and light green water.

Returned to camp as another shower dampened dinner. These last few days of forced inactivity were useful in as much as we were able to discover quite a few Eskimo camp remains in the near vicinity, marking this place as an ancient campsite. Numerous stone tent rings are situated in the lea of a cliff. The stones are arranged in a near perfect circle about 10' in diameter and served to anchor the outer edge of a tent. Close to the area, we also found a stone kayak rack made of stones placed in a series of twos, forming a bench on which a boat could be placed. Stone-lined holes, perhaps for storing meat, were nearby, and I picked up what seems to be the coaming of a large kayak.

Peter | SEPTEMBER 3, DUBAWNT RIVER

Raining again this morning. It's more a heavy mist than rain, blowing along close to the ground. Still a strong wind too and very cold. Art and I talked about making the portage on this side of the river, starting this afternoon, but I don't think anything will come of it. Art is full of talk about traveling rapidly now that the weather is cold, but I think he is one of the slowest and laziest among us. He always manages to rationalize us out of traveling when he doesn't feel like it.

After lunch Skip and I got empty pack sacks and walked down river to gather driftwood. It is quite abundant in some spots and we had no trouble filling our bags. It is quite easy to stay warm once you get out and do something, but sitting around camp, the chill settles in again quickly enough.

The fishing is fantastic when you hit a good spot. Just before dinner, I made four casts and got three fine trout. They are in lovely shape with lots of fat under the skin.

Skip | SEPTEMBER 4, DUBAWNT RIVER

Snow greeted me this morning as I crawled out of the tent into a harsh flurry. A tiny drift had accumulated on the leeward side of the tent and the rocks and moss were all covered with fine flakes. Water bucket was frozen solid and throughout the preparation of breakfast, I was working in the face of flurries.

After breakfast, we loaded in the snow, shot one rapid in the midst of a heavy flurry and then unloaded for the long portage.

By lunch the skies had cleared and the sun warmed things considerably.

Canoes were carried along the rim of the gorge in dazzling sunshine . . . many photos; a sight I'll never forget. The dark, unmovable stone walls meeting with sudden violence the infinite power of the river, foaming white against solid black rock; thrashing turquoise against swirling blue and foaming ice-green water exploding into dancing bubbles, finally disappearing in a misty rainbow. The river finally breaks its bonds and flows gently into Grant Lake, stretching 8–10 miles to the north.

Weather permitting, we will complete the portage tomorrow and, after a parting visit, leave this magnificent spot.

Peter | SEPTEMBER 4, DUBAWNT RIVER

Very cold last night and this morning. There was thick ice on the water bucket and lots of snow coming down in flurries all during breakfast. It still melts when it hits the ground, but at the rate we are going, it probably will be staying there by the time we arrive at Baker.

After a lot of fussing around with his camera, Art finally got ready and we pulled over to the other side and stopped to look over the last rapid before the portage started. We ran it close to the right side, but by the time that we got through and over to the head of the portage, it was 2:00 and time for lunch.

It is still cold sitting around, but the clouds are breaking up some and a little sun is getting through. There was no wind, so we took over the canoes, getting one load each across this afternoon, except for Art who took pictures of the portage. It was really quite beautiful. The sky cleared up completely and the portage was almost all dry. A pleasant walk over open prairie with the rapids thundering along all white among the black rocks. At one point, about half way, there is a sandy plateau and from here you can look back and see the rapids for about a mile; a white narrow stream cutting through the rocks. Then about even with the plateau, it becomes slower with big beautiful green pools, a fall of a few feet, then another pool. Finally it spreads out and runs into Grant Lake over a shallows.

The most beautiful portage I have ever made and the most beautiful spot on the river so far. To the north, the hills behind Grant Lake are all red with dwarf birch, some of them quite steep and rugged for this country.

After the cold stormy weather we have been having, this break was delightful and everyone was in high spirits and full of good predictions about the weather for the rest of the trip. Even I am not in such a hurry to move now, though I know I am getting later and later for college every day. There is almost no chance that I will make it on time now.

It gets quite cold when the sun goes down, even though this is a relatively warm evening. Everyone goes to bed early.

Skip | SEPTEMBER 5, GRANT LAKE

Breaking ice in the water bucket and melting milk from the night before has become regular morning chore now. The first one-half hour before the fire is really perking and the oats cooking is pretty grim business. I certainly will appreciate coming down the stairs into a warm room with breakfast right there in front of me.

Barrenlands portage with the eighteen-foot, ninety-pound Chestnut Peterborough Prospector canoe along the Dubawnt River, vicinity Grant Lake. Courtesy Creigh Moffatt.

We spent the better part of the day completing the portage and the late afternoon killing and butchering what will probably be our last caribou. The animals have very considerately kept right with us in spite of the cold weather. The berries and mushrooms have long since shriveled and disappeared, but the caribou remain for the pot.

We are now cooking all our meals on the green dwarf birch twigs and have pretty well worked into the laborious collecting and stoking routine.

Sugar ration has been cut again, while Art continues to snitch.

Memo for future trips: load up on starches and seasoning, and easy on the meat. We have plenty of meat but very little else and after an extended period even great quantities of meat are not very satisfying.

Wool sweater supplements long underwear and pajamas at night.

Peter | SEPTEMBER 5, GRANT LAKE

Still sunny this morning, but cold. A heavy layer of ice on the water bucket as there has been for the last few days. I got underway right after breakfast and got my two loads across long before lunch. Again, Art is the only one holding up the works with two more loads to go by lunch.

After lunch, it started to cloud over from the north, but it was still quite calm. Still Art was taking so long that we decided not to travel this afternoon, but to camp here at the end of the portage and kill a caribou; not a particularly wise thing in my mind as good traveling weather is becoming awfully scarce.

Still, I settled down to enjoy the afternoon by fishing. I had caught only three tiny trout and grayling in an hour and was about to give up, but tried one more pool and hooked an enormous Arctic char on my first cast. I played him for at least half an hour, and he went a shade under 15 lb. We had this fish for dinner and he was enough for the six of us. Bruce came in about the same time I landed the fish saying he had shot a caribou and he went back to butcher it.

Things have turned cold and cloudy with thunder showers again, so we are back in the Arctic autumn once more.

Skip | SEPTEMBER 6, GRANT LAKE AT CHAMBERLIN RIVER

Got a late start this morning due to our unconscious reluctance to head out amid cold, driving snow. But after an hour or so of vigorous paddling, we were warm enough to really enjoy a cold, brisk and remarkably refreshing day.

First off, Bruce and I shot a rocky rapid flowing into the lake. We struck a rock just after leaving shore and were able to stop in an eddy to check for damage; and when a brief check showed no water, we started out again, this time making it with no trouble.

Art and Pete watched from shore. Art chose to portage. Pete shot the rapid, hit a rock in the shoals below and splintered a plank.

A heavy wind out of the North kept us from making any real progress and after a lunch of hardtack, etc., and tea, we were pushed against the shore.

About 4 PM we spotted a large animal on a nearby ridge and after cautiously approaching the shore, we were all thrilled to see our first barren ground grizzly. This is a tremendous animal, especially at this season just before hibernation. He must weigh at least as much as a horse, extremely thick throughout his forward body; a prominent hump just forward of his shoulder emphasizes his huge neck and powerful forequarters and a beautiful late-season coat, shimmering and rippling, even in the dull light of the snow laden sky. A light-colored area begins on each shoulder and extends forward down each foreleg to the gigantic paws. The total appearance is one of tremendous power coupled with amazing agility.

Art, of course, was wrapped around his telephoto lens and while the rest remained in the canoes, I followed behind Art with the Leica. Quite a comical pantomime, the bear grazing from bush to bush with the unconcern of complete confidence and two rather cautious, crouching forms approaching with noses glued to cameras. It was wonderful; we got very close before he saw us and then he merely looked, sat down, "thought it over," ambled closer to satisfy his curiosity, and then making a tremendous picture silhouetted full length against the sky to examine these strange intruders. We played ring around each other for a while until the bear worked downwind of us and within 100' or so: Then instead of running from the human scent, he continued right for us. Rather than be caught with the bear between us and the canoes, Art and I ran for the shore, and this sudden movement was enough to turn the bear and send him scampering over the rocks along the shore and out of sight.

Made camp at the mouth of the Chamberlin River and were happily surprised to find large quantities of driftwood. Have plenty for morning in addition to two full packsacks which we will carry with us and hoard as long as possible.

When we unloaded the canoe, I found that the morning rock had splintered the planking and cracked a rib pretty badly, so the few remaining hours of daylight were spent in makeshift repair. I certainly enjoy this crude carpentry. Hope my future has an old fence or something that will call for a little puttering.

Peter | SEPTEMBER 6, GRANT LAKE AT CHAMBERLIN RIVER

Cold and rainy; only a slight mist though. I took a walk after breakfast to warm up and noticed the wind was quite high and against us on Grant

Lake, but Art decided to travel just the same. He hung in his tent long after the rest of us were ready to go, so we didn't leave until 11:00. Skip and I decided to shoot down through what was left of the rapid into Grant, while Art made a portage and started further down to warm up. Skip went first, but struck against a rock at the head of the rapid. He got the rest of the way down and started paddling up against the wind, so apparently no great damage was done. I shoved off and got further out in the middle, but I struck head on and bounced over a rock about half way down. It sounded awful, but when we looked later, we found that there was a little piece of the planking knocked in, but the ribs weren't broken and the canvas wasn't cut; no serious damage. The rest of the rapid was all dangerously shoal with barely enough water for the canoe, but we got through all right. Skip and I pulled up to wait for Art and had lunch when he joined us. Then we shoved off and started up the shore again. Progress was heartbreakingly slow as the wind was dead against us.

We had gone maybe 1.5 mi. when we saw a barren ground grizzly on the shore; an enormous bear with silvery fur around the shoulders. He had a thick layer of fat built up already and shimmered all over when he moved. We pulled over right away and Skip and Art got out to get pictures. Before he saw us, he was wandering around in a lazy way feeding on the hillside every now and then. He would sit down on his seat, just like a toy bear, and look around in a most comic way. When he did see Art and Skip, he got up right away and started walking over to see what we were. All of a sudden, he started running toward us and Art was so nervous, he could hardly work the camera. When he got fairly close, he stopped and stood up on his hind legs to have a better look at us. He certainly seemed enormous and he probably tried to get downwind of us. The wind was blowing right toward us off the land, because he walked down to the shore and on to a spit of land just below us, about 50 yd. away. Finally something scared him and he took off over the hills at a terrific pace. A man could never keep away from him by running, if he charged. He got out of sight in no time at all.

Then Art settled down close to a ptarmigan to wait for the sun, while George shot two others. When I got ready to clean them, I found my knife was gone, then remembered I had used it last at lunch and must have left it there, so back I went at a half-run, half-walk and found it there. On my way back, I picked up a good bundle of driftwood.

After we left this spot, we fought the headwinds for another two or three miles and then decided to camp at the mouth of the Chamberlin River. Tyrrell said that there were willows on this river and sure enough, when I walked up wood gathering, I found them. Some were at least ten feet tall, but they were low down by the water and there was no dry, dead wood on them; all green. When I came back to the mouth of the river, Bruce had been gathering driftwood there and had quite a pile. I guess all of the dead wood gets washed down by the Spring floods and is left in the eddy at the mouth of the river. Working together, Bruce and I filled three pack sacks with good wood, in addition to what we needed for dinner and breakfast; enough for three days if we are careful. Still overcast and quite cold when we turned in, but not windy.

Skip | SEPTEMBER 7, GRANT LAKE

This warm, sunny morning was replaced by a sudden squall just about the time we were ready to pull out, and we spent the next few hours until after lunch huddled under our canoes while the driving rain and damp cold slowly seeped into our bones. While sitting there, the question of traveling in the rain was kicked around in a variety of terms; most revolving around the uncomfortable, immediate situation, the vague possibility of freezing our feet if we remained in this country for very much longer, and the fuel supply. But the sun soon appeared before anything was decided and we moved on half-helped and half-hindered by a gusty West wind.

Five miles later, we spotted a cache of oil drums on the far shore which upon closer inspection turned out to be the remnants of Ray Moore's last camp. Along with the gasoline, also found a large quantity of dehydrated vegetables. I was very disappointed in the general lack of respect for a cache which the guys showed here. No thought whatsoever was given to the possible purpose of the supplies, only the self-centered joy of finding more food. Turns out some vague mention of leftovers had passed between Art and Ray in Ottawa and so we took the whole shebang. Hope a wandering Eskimo doesn't go hungry.

Saw three beautiful white wolves on a nearby ridge early in the day. They certainly look well-fed.

Peter | SEPTEMBER 7, GRANT LAKE

Cloudy and a strong wind from the northwest. Cold as usual. Skip found that he had a broken rib when he hit a rock in the last rapid, and so he patched that up this morning. On top of a steep esker across the river from camp, we saw three white wolves right after breakfast. They stood there in silhouette against the skyline for quite some time. This hill is only about 200 or 300 yd. from camp and I could see them quite clearly. Art was going to go over and take pictures, but then it clouded in heavily, so we decided to pull out and travel instead. Unfortunately, just as George and I finished loading and shoved off, it started to rain and everyone else got under Skip's canoe which was still on shore. We came back and piled under it before it really started and waited for something to happen. It just kept on, so after an hour, we started to debate about traveling in the rain. George, I and Art for; the rest against.

At last the rain stopped before we could reach any conclusion, so we had lunch and got going. When we reached the foot of the big esker at the mouth of the river, we saw some red gas drums on the beach and pulled over. Behind them, we found a cache of dried vegetables apparently left there by Ray Moore. We tried the gas cans and found a little, but all leaded, which would clog the stove, but George said that he used Coleman stoves with leaded gas in the Army and they worked for at least 10 hours before clogging, so we filled our five-gallon can and put the remaining white gas in jam cans.

It looked like rain, so we decided to camp at the end of a narrow bay cutting back into the esker. From the cache we had gotten twenty-four enormous cans of dried vegetables, more than we could possibly eat. We tried cooking one can for dinner and it filled two pots by the time we got all the meat and a handful of Catelli in. We started eating with relish, but the vegetables soon palled and only Joe could finish what was left. Even he nearly got sick that night. I don't care if I never see another vegetable, except onions; I still crave them.

Skip | SEPTEMBER 8, WHARTON LAKE

AM. Rainy breakfast and the prospect of clearing skies in the near future send us to the tents for a lazy, relatively calm wait. Bruce is curled up in his sleeping bag beside me; heavy breathing and a few irregular snorts indicate a contented post-breakfast snooze. I sit, half crouched against my rolled-up sleeping bag with the air mattress beneath me for protection against the cold ground and an occasional puddle of water which accumulated in the numerous depressions on the floor during a night of steady rain. Caribou hide draped over my legs and feet. Small droplets of water condense on the inside of the tent and run in tiny streams down to the floor while the smoke from my stoking pipe rises slowly into a bluish cloud along the ridge pole. Partially dry socks and shirts lay along the edges of the floor after spending another night in my sleeping bag during the long and not too successful process of drying. My boots have by this time become more like well-used sponges than any resemblance to leather, and as the days go on, the sole gradually separates from the disintegrating stitches. We are all pretty much in the same boat; no one boot standing the tough treatment any better than the others. Consequently our feet are always cold and the stinging ache of damp cold is as much a part of the routine as anything else; will certainly enjoy toasting dry feet in front of a roaring fire once again.

Our little candle "stove" is flickering between us now, sending long shadows darting across the white fluttering walls; it seems as if the wind is freshening and the rain has stopped. So we will pack up soon (I hope) and be on our way.

PM. Intermittent showers kept us in camp until 4 PM, but we were able to wander about somewhat between the rains and found quite an extensive archaeological site. None of us are experts by any means, but we have been picking up the most obvious specimens and by now can distinguish some distinctive characteristics. We're also generally able to recognize fragments of implements from mere chippings. It is interesting to note how the quality of the tool changes as it becomes more recent. High up on an old wave-cut bank the work is near perfect while lower down on more recent beaches the pieces seem less complex, more crude.

Before we left the States, Art had arranged that Elmer Harp, Dartmouth Archaeology Faculty, would have a look at whatever we could collect, so we'll learn more after he has finished with whatever we can bring back.

The highlight of our wanderings for me was a musk ox skull complete with horns, which I found in a grassy meadow high on the main esker of the region. Hope I will be able to pack it out during the rest of the trip.

We are camped above a rocky rapid on a very exposed boulder plain and as I write, the wind and driving snow-rain intensifies. The tent shudders and the nearby "tarp-cook house" flaps violently. Sleep tonight will be restless at best.

Peter | SEPTEMBER 8, WHARTON LAKE

Cloudy and cold this morning. After breakfast, Art and I spent nearly the whole morning looking for artifacts on the esker. At beach level, Art found traces of an old oven or a cooking hole, along with a few points. Then we looked over the high part of the esker and on the very summit, I found a few points, one fine small arrowhead and a blade, along with quite a few fragments of other arrowheads.

TROUBLE

TYRRELL, 1893	LOCATION	MOFFATT, 1955
August 7–17	Dubawnt Lake	August 21–27
TOTAL: 32 days		TOTAL: 51 days
August 22	Wharton Lake	September 8
August 29	Schultz Lake	September 22

From here until 9/17 our daily, chronologic journal entries end. The days after 9/8 were filled with such horror and suffering that it was impossible to write anything at all. In one moment, this grand adventure had become a nightmare beyond my comprehension. The narrative that follows was written after we had arrived at Baker Lake, after the others had departed and I was alone with my recollections and my demons. —*Skip*

AS THE STORM OF EARLY LAST NIGHT GREW in severity, the rain changed to wet, clinging snow and after a few hours the ground, rocks, tents, every solid projection, were covered with frozen, caked snow. The wind is so strong that it is impossible to hold the tarp flys over the tents; they are torn away in an instant. The combination of wind and the weight of collecting snow collapsed our tent so that Bruce and I huddled in the middle with the cold, wet sides plastered against me. My side of the tent was almost completely collapsed so that I lay with the wet, slapping roof pushed down on my face. Bruce's side was blown out like a balloon and threatened to take off or burst at any minute. Once during the night, we heard faint shouting and after calling repeatedly, we heard an answer, "We're all right; completely soaked." Our fear of getting wet and frostbitten had increased with each day of rain/snow, near-freezing temperatures and high winds; and now with the blizzard howling outside, Bruce and I crawled into our soggy bags, shivering with cold and apprehension.

Our consolation is that snow, like rain, has an end sometime and we only need to hold out, using as little food as possible, until it stops. I began writing this morning to take my mind off the storm, but now my hands are so cold that I can no longer hold the pencil properly, so back into the bag for more long, uncertain hours. What earlier in the night were abrupt efforts to dodge the mounting puddles and wet walls in the tent have now become rather pitiful twitches of numb unconcern as we lay half in icy water, half in relative dryness.

The wind abated but continued to blow later in the morning and with faint daylight softening the fury of the storm, I crawled to the tent opening and peered out. The landscape had changed remarkably during the night. What before had been black, rugged rock was now gray, glistening ice. Puddles were frozen and the ground covered with harsh, windblown snow. The river rushed by, gray and heavy, disappearing into dirty yellow foam at the rapids. The wind blew stinging swirls of snow against my face and tore at the tent guy lines as I gazed around camp, looking for some sign of the others. One tent was demolished, with broken poles and badly torn fabric. The other tent was collapsed and half buried in snow. I shouted again. This time a faint call came from under one of the overturned canoes. There under a pile of canvas and wet sleeping bags were Pete and George. Their tent had been torn apart early in the storm and they had spent the rest of the night huddled under the canoe. Together we dug out the other tent and found Art and Joe perched on a pile of wet clothes in the middle of a puddle. They had pitched their tent in a small depression; soon it flooded and then collapsed under the weight of the wet, wind-driven snow.

It took us three days to recover from this blizzard and from then on the tempo of the trip changed. We were dazed. It had been cold before, and uncomfortable, but never so sudden and so furious. Our equipment was not intended for such conditions, our minds were not accustomed to traveling in snow flurries with ice forming in the quiet pools at river's edge and on our paddles with each stroke. Yet there was no thought of turning back; we were beyond that both geographically and emotionally.

Up at daylight; four men breaking camp, the other two preparing breakfast of oatmeal with a carefully rationed teaspoon of sugar and a cup of tea, then into the canoes. Every hour we stopped, crawled stiffly out of the canoes and ran up and down the rocky shore until the circulation returned to warm and sting our numb feet. Then off again, racing northward in the swift current. Snow flurries were frequent; the temperature usually near freezing; the wind blew incessantly. But there was an occasional break in the leaden sky when the sun warmed us briefly. We still had time to get out.

We left camp late in the morning on Sept. 14 and after completing a short portage, loaded the canoes and continued our dash down the river. It was cold and windy; the sky was overcast and we stopped at frequent intervals to warm our feet and legs.

We had lunch about 3 PM and then pushed on, anxious to reach Marjorie Lake, about ten miles away, before nightfall. As the river approaches this lake, its channel is broken into many narrow riffles by small, low islands. We traveled quickly and steadily, shooting past the tiny islets, hesitating briefly at the top of each riffle to check the water ahead and quickly pick a course through the swift water. By now we were accustomed to the ways of the river and approached what we thought must be the last rapids with confidence and impatience. Art stood up in his drifting canoe, looked ahead, and then sat down and drove his canoe for the middle of the flow.

I followed, then Pete and George, and soon all three canoes were gliding down the smooth water of the upper rapid. We reached a bend in the rapids; Art's canoe disappeared. The next thing I saw as we shot around the bend was a white wall of huge waves directly in our path. Beyond the thundering waves, the yellow camera box and Art's gray canoe bobbed crazily in the rapids below.

"Art's tipped over," Bruce shouted and turned to look questioningly at me. I glanced quickly to shore and for a moment thought we could reach a small eddy near the bank; but in another instant, before we could fight our way out of the rushing current, the waves were on us.

"Hold her steady," I shouted as we smashed into the first wave. The bow dipped and Bruce disappeared in a crash of foam. The canoe stopped, shuddered, and then slowly regained speed. Water rushed over the duffel and swirled around my knees. We were still afloat. I fought the sluggish canoe in a futile attempt to avoid the second wave. All I could do was keep the canoe straight and hope we would somehow miss the second blow. Solid water hit us hard and rushed over us. The canoe settled quietly and slowly turned over. Cold water hit me like a punch in the stomach. I was breathless. It was not a sensation of cold, nothing hurt; just a sudden shock and then numbness.

We clung to the canoe as it slowly drifted into a small bay at the bottom of the rapids and dumbly watched Pete and George struggle toward shore with their swamped canoe. They dumped the water out and paddled furiously back toward us. Long, dull minutes passed and by this time Art and Joe had drifted into quiet water below the rapid. They floated ahead of us clutching the canoe with only their heads and arms above water. Art had one arm over the gunwale, the other holding the camera box.

At last a canoe was next to us. George reached out for my arm, wrenched my hand free of its numb grasp and clamped my fingers over the gunwale of his canoe; then a slow drag toward shore. My feet bumped against a slippery rock; the canoe stopped and I was released. Bruce stumbled and fell stiffly into the shallow water beside me. I took a step forward and lurched against an icy rock. Somehow we crawled out of the water, regained our footing and stood in dumb silence while Art and Joe were dragged ashore. When we reached them they were both delirious, sprawled stiff and grotesque on the frozen tundra.

Shivering violently, our limbs stiff and numb, we managed to tear the frozen clothing off Art and Joe, wrap them in soggy sleeping bags and as much dry clothing as we had. Pete got a small fire going and we carried Art close to it and then set up a tent and put Joe in it with George.

Back at the fire with Art . . . massage, more blankets, a brief struggle and then the shaking stopped. George came out of the tent and struggled into the bag with Art. "There's no pulse. I can't hear a heart beat," George whispered to me, his head pressed against Art's slender chest.

"No! Try again!" Nothing.

It had happened so quickly, seemingly so easily; no violence, nothing dramatic; a brief struggle and then an empty finality.

I looked at Art again. I'm not sure what I saw nor what I expected to see, but it seemed that in his face the harshness and suffering of the last few hours had relaxed into a calm peacefulness. Perhaps the spirit of adventure and pioneering, the necessity to live in harmony with Nature and the insistence that simplicity in living is the key to an understanding of life had not defeated him, it had received him.

Hardly conscious of what we were doing or what had happened, Pete and I picked up Art's body and placed it in the shelter of a large rock.

The five of us spent the night in the remaining tent, shivering in wet sleeping bags, whispering cautiously of how it had happened and why, when we were so near the end; afraid of the night and what the morning might bring. Joe slowly regained consciousness and then fell into a deep slumber.

We spent the next two days collecting the remains of our equipment, drying our clothes and trying to re-establish some kind of emotional stability. We had lost our leader, our mentor; both rifles, all our cooking equipment and most of our food, but we had a plan.

We would travel in two canoes, moving slowly to conserve our strength. Instead of continuing down the Dubawnt and risking another dangerous rapid before Beverly Lake and into Aberdeen Lake, we would portage eight miles from Marjorie Lake to the central portion of Aberdeen Lake and the Thelon River, then head for the trading post at Baker Lake.

With a plan to follow, we focused on the problems of traveling and the business of survival, trying to ignore our loss and forget the horror of the last few days. We built a small cairn on the summit of the island, leaving behind the broken canoe, our cameras, film, the completed maps, and Art.

Skip | SEPTEMBER 17, MARJORIE LAKE, DUBAWNT RIVER

Even after only one day of travel since leaving our emergency camp, we have evolved into a relatively smooth working unit. It is heartening to see how the guys are cooperating and helping. We all feel very much indebted to each other and are thankful to be alive.

We get up as a group at 6 AM; while Bruce and George cook breakfast, Joe, Pete and I break camp and load the canoes so that immediately after eating we are ready to leave. Our food consists of some cans of meat which were salvaged, a quantity of wet oats and corn meal, some dehydrated veggies, and, of course, fish (we were lucky to have saved one casting rod). Breakfast then generally involves a mixture of wet oats, fish and some milk powder cooked in a sort of pasty stew. The rest of the meals are pretty much the same, although lunches are the usual fare of hardtack, etc. (these items having survived in Pete's canoe). Dinner is generally a repeat of breakfast, with perhaps a chunk of bacon boiled in the stew. We are using large veggie cans to cook in and are eating out of tobacco tins and using knives and sticks of wood for utensils. We are extremely lucky to have been able to improvise this way, in as much as all our cooking equipment has been lost and we are quite happy with the caveman style. The food is all paste, horrible looking, and probably the most welcome dishes these five have ever had.

After camping last night in a rather uncertain state of mind as to our position, I'm getting used to navigating with our limited maps, and now, after completing a good days travel and having arrived at our intended destination, my navigating confidence is growing and I think we can find our way through to Baker.

Tomorrow we will tackle the eight mile trek from the NE arm of Marjorie Lake to the south shore of Aberdeen Lake. I spent two hours after we landed this evening scouting our probable route and after getting a glimpse of the distant lake from a high hill, was able to establish what I hope will be a relatively direct and dry route.

We have abandoned all but the most essential personal effects; divided up the food and are set to go. Two men will each carry a pack plus one canoe. George, as the extra man, will carry the one wooden box we have retained, filled with the more fragile food supplies and those which would ruin the personal packs. We plan to spend the entire day on the portage, walking together and stopping to rest as frequently as necessary. I only

Tyrrell

[T]he next day we pushed on to Aberdeen Lake . . . That evening I called the men together and told them that they had a long journey yet before them, that the summer flowers had all withered, and that winter would very soon be on us.

hope that youth, determination and luck will combine tomorrow to see us through this severe test. Early to bed should help immensely.

Skip | SEPTEMBER 18, THE BIG TREK

Our start this morning was delayed almost until noon because we couldn't fit two guys with packs under one canoe. We finally had to carry the canoes singly and be satisfied with making an extra trip for the remaining packs.

So we started off. At first we tried to stick to the firm ridges with relatively dry feet, but the ridges soon became too diverse and the feet too wet for any special detour. Broken boulder mazes alternated with low grassy swamps in which the puddles were covered with ice. A strong southerly wind made carrying the canoes particularly difficult, often spinning the canoe completely around and twisting the carrier down into the mud. Wet feet cracking ice and plunging into cold water, then to stumble and stagger on sharp, ragged rocks; shoulders ache, back straining, legs plodding in numb confusion.

After deciding to leave the canoe for the night, I picked up our remaining food box and pushed on with Bruce toward the lake. It was getting dark and as we approached a group of small ponds near which we intended to camp, we encountered a pack of four wolves. We first saw them sitting directly in front of us and as we grew nearer, one remained sitting; the others moved off on each side of our path in what seemed like an obvious and planned encirclement. We kept walking, expecting our scent to scare them off, but soon became concerned when we got within 30 yards or so and the one in front of us remained motionless. It was an unusual impulse to try and scare off wild animals instead of coaxing them nearer, but we didn't hesitate, started yelling and waving our arms. It worked. The wolves turned and ran, disappearing over a nearby ridge.

Bruce and I continued for a short distance and then made camp on the bank of a low, swampy pond about a mile from the south shore of Aberdeen Lake. We expected the others to arrive while we were setting camp, but no one appeared; so while Bruce stayed in camp working on a hot soup, I retraced our steps, and it wasn't until I had gone all the way back to our canoe that I met the others, strung out among the low hills. I picked up another pack and trudged into camp completely played out; threw down Bruce's fine soup and crawled in.

Earlier in the day, I realized I lost my gloves during the many stops and starts and went back over the maze of rocks and swamp to find them, but no luck. I don't want to hold up our good progress because of my stupidity, so I'll finish the trip with woolen socks wrapped around my hands, and hope for warm weather.

This portage saved us time and protected against our fear of heavy rapids and another potential accident. My confidence is gaining that we have a good chance to make it. If the weather will hold fair for a few more days; if our bodies can hold up under the strain of poor food and hard work; if we can keep calm and act with clear, steady action and never again let anticipation and haste override caution; if . . .

Skip | SEPTEMBER 19, BIG TREK, ABERDEEN LAKE

Sun, south wind, ice melting on some puddles; the staggering march across the Marjorie Hills continued, accentuated by the sore muscles and tender bruises of yesterday. Our feet are probably in the worst condition, blistered and soft from the continual exposure to ice water and sharp rocks. Pete and I doubled up on one canoe this morning and arrived back at camp for breakfast in rather bad shape, certain that we needed two on each canoe for the rest of the portage. So after breakfast, George and Joe went back for the other canoe while Pete and I headed again for the distant lake. Left the canoe at the shore; back for another load; quick lunch; and then into the canoes again. With a strong south wind at our tail, we managed to reach the north shore of the lake before dusk.

Made camp in a beautiful, sheltered, sandy lagoon and fell asleep with relief, pride and satisfaction of having just crossed our own special Atlantic. We all feel now that it is only a matter of time before we reach the outpost; all the big obstacles seem to be over . . . crossed fingers.

Ever since we dragged each other out of that miserable tent on the cloudy morning of the 15th, we have been blessed with warm, sunny

Tyrrell

We continued our journey eastward, losing one day in a search for the outlet of Aberdeen Lake, and two days from a heavy storm, until on September 2 we reached the west end of Baker Lake. . . . We had now accomplished our journey through the unknown interior country, and gained the first recognizable point since leaving Black Lake, 810 miles behind us.

weather with a continual south wind to dry us, warm us and, above all, renew our confidence in our chances of survival. Dry clothes and sufficient dry twigs for an occasional warm meal have helped tremendously, and the country and the elements at least seem neutral again, instead of stacked against us.

Now that the great Marjorie-Aberdeen trek has been completed, I can view with a little less alarm the sad state of my boots. The sole of the left one has completely torn off the upper boot. This happened many weeks ago, and I had been able to hold the two together with tacks, string and brass wire. But now the middle portion of leather finally disintegrated, leaving nothing to attach the two and so I clump along with a soggy sock sticking out and a very cold toe. The right shoe is in a little better shape, but so spongy and soft that it affords little more protection than a foot wrapping. The luxury of warm feet and hands will always be dear to me after this.

Skip | SEPTEMBER 20, ABERDEEN LAKE

It seems that our exceptional period of good weather has finally come to an end, although we were able to get in a full day of travel today before the rains came. We woke up this morning to a brilliant red, gold dawn with a dark cloud bank to the west. The south wind shifted to the east, but was very mild, and we left this cozy little bay at 8:30 AM under uncertain skies and the ominous warning of "Red skies at morning . . ." The wind died completely in the PM and we traveled on borrowed time during the lull.

My navigation got a severe test today and panic nearly overcame me for a while. We were traveling along an uninterrupted coast in sloppy seas, which made any estimate of mileage covered difficult; the sun was hidden and the map very inaccurate. It seemed like hours that we spent looking for the outlet bay from Aberdeen Lake. Each little point would build up my hopes and then peter out in a sandy beach or rocky cove. Finally, just when I was ready to declare that we were lost, I called a rest on one of the points and climbed a tiny ridge. There to the northeast, the entire outlet stretched before my eyes and I knew that we were nearly finished with this huge body of water; from the depths of gloom and confusion to the heights of exhilaration in a minute.

We continued into the bay and soon spotted a white, glistening tent on the western shore; paddled over, and saw our first Eskimo family and first human beings in almost three months. Only women and children were in camp and the five of us stood awkwardly in front of a woman and three children. Sign language seems particularly useless between genders, unless perhaps the language of sex, and that was about the farthest from our minds as we looked at the bundled, pudgy figures. The youngest child was completely sewed in a caribou suit; boots, gloves, hood, all in one; don't see how they ever got him out of it.

We made camp a few miles from the family tent and were visited by the husband and two boys in their kicker canoe returning from a hunting trip. Very friendly; traded knives for tobacco; gave them chocolate bars and dehydrated vegetables; sorry we couldn't offer better presents, but by the looks of them, they are in much better shape than we are. Rain started falling as we waved goodbye, and we crawled into our tents hoping for another day or so of traveling weather to see us to our destination.

Definite changes in the attitude of the guys; emergency is generally considered over and once again the warmth of the sleeping bag dictates morning lethargy. I really have to prod and hustle in the early hours. When the Eskimo first drifted their canoe on to the beach, our first hesitating question concerned Baker Lake . . . direction? distance? He pointed to the east and raised one finger (day?). Then he looked at our canoes, picked up a paddle, laughed; paused a moment as if thinking back to those earlier days of canoe paddling, and raised 3 fingers. So three days of travel to the end. After such a long time, it's easy to understand the relaxation.

Fall Clothing of the Dubawnt Eskimo: Knee-high rubber boots, or lightweight seal-skin mukluks, with a ragged pair of canvas trousers tucked into them. Through the holes in this outer layer I could see the khaki-colored wool of GI trousers as an inner layer. Summer parka was made of rather light, faintly striped cotton material with the usual pointed hood, but no fur lining; all topped off with a plaid, peaked hat with ear flaps. The younger boys generally dressed the same except that the outer trousers are of the same material as the parka. The women also wear a parka and skirt (over how many layers?) of this summer material, but seem to favor canvas or seal-skin moccasins. Everyone has bright red cheeks, which is so characteristic of the Albany River Indians and does not seem to be necessarily characteristic of good health; too bright, unnatural.

Skip | SEPTEMBER 21, ABERDEEN LAKE

The rain of last night changed to snow sometime during the windblown darkness. The favoring wind of the past few days has shifted to a strong headwind from the east. All this combined with the relative security of our campsite convinced us to remain in camp until the weather eases. And so we are in the tents; Bruce, Pete and I jammed in one, George and Joe in the other. We just finished our bad-weather breakfast of one hardtack with a spoonful of jam and will now probably doze and sleep until clearing, or at least until everyone gets tired enough of the cramped quarters to want to venture out into the snow.

We continue spending a cold, impatient day in camp. Plans to move immediately after lunch were thwarted because Bruce had some difficulty getting the food going until 2 PM. I took a long walk after the meal to stretch legs and settle temper. Reached a high ridge south of camp and from there was able to see our route eastward almost to Schultz Lake. Intervening ranges of snow-covered ridges and intermittent snow flurries make it seem a long way off, but if I can keep the gang going for a few more days, we will make it.

Returned now to the tent where I have just completed rechecking our credentials, money, and customs clearances. Baker Lake looms as the end of one adventure and the beginning of another. I hope I can handle the complications of Art's death in the proper manner. But first things first, and my mind is still full of weather, navigation and travel; luckily it still has not room for the inevitable retrospection of our accident.

Just as we were finishing a cold dinner of a chunk of so-called canned ham and a few apricots in our tents, we were hailed from outside by our Eskimo friend of yesterday. "Come, my canoe, tea," he said in broken English, punctuated by many gestures and smiles.

Not knowing exactly what was in store for us, we bundled up and followed this happy fellow who finally introduced himself with a big smile, "Me Alec Itscha, Itscha, Itscha."

On the way to the canoe, Alec showed off his waterproof mukluks by running nimbly through the icy water near the shore. Fur on the inside, hide on the outside with beautifully sewn seams at the ankle, and tied just below the knee. We countered enviously with our tattered tailor-mades and all laughed.

On the other side of the hill, Alec's son and another young boy had a primus stove set up in a canvas-draped crate and were busy making tea. After we arrived, Alec jumped into the large freight canoe pulled up on the shore and came back with a huge kettle of caribou chunks. Meat and wonderful stewing broth after all these days of lean meals! It was marvelous. We stood around chewing on the chunks, drinking tea and talking with smiles and gestures. This was Alec's way of repaying our meager hospitality of last night. Before we left, I ran back to camp and picked up a spare paddle, which I gave to him. He was delighted. On the way back, I learned that the afternoon had included heated discussions of how stupid it was for Skip to give our last four chocolate bars to that Eskimo. Now everyone was glad; returned to bed full and very happy with our new friends.

Skip | SEPTEMBER 22, THELON RIVER, SCHULTZ LAKE

The boredom and frustrated anticipation of yesterday led us out of the tents at 5 AM, and by 7 AM we were on our way. The morning warmed

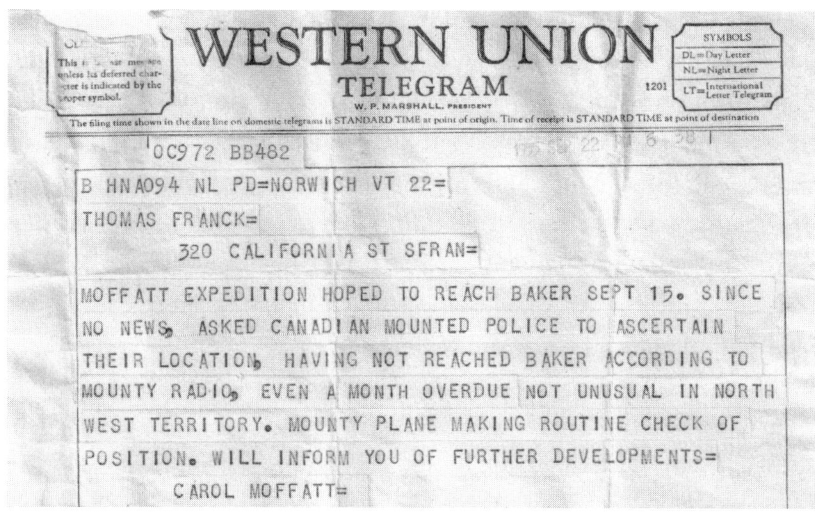

WESTERN UNION
TELEGRAM
W. P. MARSHALL, PRESIDENT

SYMBOLS
DL=Day Letter
NL=Night Letter
LT=International Letter Telegram

1201

The filing time shown in the date line on domestic telegrams is STANDARD TIME at point of origin. Time of receipt is STANDARD TIME at point of destination

OC972 BB482

B HNA094 NL PD=NORWICH VT 22=
THOMAS FRANCK=
320 CALIFORNIA ST SFRAN=

MOFFATT EXPEDITION HOPED TO REACH BAKER SEPT 15. SINCE NO NEWS, ASKED CANADIAN MOUNTED POLICE TO ASCERTAIN THEIR LOCATION, HAVING NOT REACHED BAKER ACCORDING TO MOUNTY RADIO, EVEN A MONTH OVERDUE NOT UNUSUAL IN NORTH WEST TERRITORY. MOUNTY PLANE MAKING ROUTINE CHECK OF POSITION. WILL INFORM YOU OF FURTHER DEVELOPMENTS=
CAROL MOFFATT=

Telegram sent from Carol Moffatt to Thomas Franck, Peter Franck's father, on September 22. Courtesy Fay Franck.

and cleared and the wind stayed at our tail no matter how our course twisted and turned.

By lunch we had traveled almost 20 miles to the western end of Schultz Lake. Wind freshened and as we left our lunch spot, we had hopes of making another ten miles or so. Wind continued and we rode the waves, nearly surfing at times. It soon became clear that if we could stick to it, we could go the entire length of the lake. Stopped for hardtack and jam at 3 PM and then continued until 6 PM, when we reached the channel to the north and the Thelon River. This has undoubtedly been the most satisfying day of our extended push and now everyone feels that we are within spitting distance of the post. Another day and a half of travel should see us through.

Skip | SEPTEMBER 23, THELON RIVER

Dispatch of our carefully hoarded food supply was the highlight of the day. Breakfast began with two tins full of cornmeal instead of just one, one can of fish/roast beef/mashed potato glop and a large pot of tea. Even with our scanty larder we seem to have come up with a surplus. Lunch saw two extra hardtacks and a few extra spoonfuls of jam . . . great stuff. Dinner continued with spinach, canned beef glop and a batch of sweet cocoa. For the second time since the 14th we go to bed with full bellies.

Arrived at the Thelon River after a stiff paddle across the last bay of Schultz Lake against a quartering wind, and had a bit of a struggle when an uncharted rapids caught us with heavy cross chop. Again we took on water over the gunwales and bailed icy water from the bilges.

We stopped for lunch at the last marked portage of the trip. We were not quite sure we had passed all the heavy rapids on this portage, but were happily surprised when we rounded a bend and saw swift, smooth current ahead. The river winds in long, sweeping turns now with a current of maybe 10 miles per hour. The banks vary from rock and grass slopes to high steep cliffs and form a pleasant, fast-moving panorama as we sweep eagerly along toward Baker Lake.

Our camp tonight is about 35 map miles from our destination, and with a certain amount of " . . . don't count your chickens . . . ," I write this as our last night on the river.

It is too soon to say much about the trip in retrospect. The guys have held up amazingly well under the circumstances, and for such a varied, inexperienced crew that began this journey, we have become extremely compatible and comfortable. Again, I only mention in brief what is foremost in my mind now that the worries of leading the trip are almost over, the significance of our accident, and the effects of having the second most influential man in my life die in my arms begin to show. It will be a long time before this experience is fully understood. Carol and the children are constantly in my thoughts. Tomorrow, I will make whatever arrangements necessary with the Mounty to return to the Marjorie Lake cache; the first step in the long, sad journey to Norwich.

Skip | SEPTEMBER 24, THELON RIVER

Today it seemed as if the elements finally decided they had exacted a great enough toll for our passage through this country, as surely they have, and gave us a gem of a day to end our long journey. The sun rose with a quickly vanishing cloudbank and shone brightly in a clear, blue sky for the entire day.

We left camp about 8 AM after our last "tin can" meal and resumed our rapid pace on the river with the sun almost blinding us. It was a marvelous climax to the trip . . . smooth, swift water with one easy rapid to lend just enough excitement to the last push; caribou grazing on the banks, lifting their heads as if to say goodbye; clear, sparkling streams tumbling into the big river from high rocky cliffs; occasional fish nosing for the odd fly . . . all so easy and delightful.

Stopped for lunch about 10 miles from the post and then slowly paddled in, each in his own private world of relief, reluctance, memories and anticipation. If only Art could have been with us to feel these culminating moments and the thrill of a hard, fascinating journey at an end . . . if only . . .

Suddenly, the gravel bars and low sandy islands of the Thelon Delta fell away into the deep, far-reaching waters of Baker Lake. The sun sparkled off the tiny rippling waves and even the canoes seemed to strain forward in the water like tired horses anxious for the stable. We paddled along a low, grassy point with the lake stretching wide on our right. No sign of the familiar white buildings with red roofs of the HBC.

"This must be the place!"; check the map again; "but everything fits perfectly." And then, around another point, a tiny, shore-cliffed bay appeared, and on the far shore, about 3 miles distant, a row of white buildings glistened in the afternoon sun. Joe gave a shout, threw his arms over his head and then took up a furious stroke, "Goodies!"

As we grew nearer, individual buildings identified themselves, and the Baker Lake post slowly developed into what appeared to be a substantial, well-kept community. On the far left, an airstrip and some large, elongated buildings appeared. From there in a narrow line between the protecting northern cliffs and the shore came a white and green church; next the brilliant white of HBC buildings, and then the red steeple of another church.

BAKER LAKE

TYRRELL, 1893	LOCATION	MOFFATT, 1955
September 2	Baker Lake (arrival)	September 24
TOTAL: 58 days		TOTAL: 85 days

Skip | SEPTEMBER 24

We were met by Corporal Clair Dent of the RCMP [Royal Canadian Mounted Police] and a host of the local population, and were quickly informed that the Air Force and local authorities were to have started a search for us this very day. Apparently the news of our overdue arrival was spread over much of the Territories. A regularly scheduled flight of Arctic Airways landed shortly after our canoes hit the shore, and within one-half hour my companions of the last three months were airborne for Churchill, leaving me behind to attend the recovery of our cache and Art.

I was taken in tow by the Corporal and after a fine cup of coffee was given a bit of a nudge toward a real bathtub with plenty of hot water . . . what a luxurious sensation! It'll take plenty more than one application of the suds to really clean up, but nevertheless I feel wonderfully peppy and much less greasy.

Treat followed treat; fresh pear, music, Sophia Loren on the cover of *Life,* and then a fine dinner of scalloped potatoes, ham with pineapple rings, string beans, fresh bread and butter, and hot minced pie.

From here we went visiting to another couple's house, Bob and Rita, radio operator, for a glass of beer, chatter and many tomato/lettuce sandwiches.

Also present was Sandy Lunan, post manager and his clerk, Jim, and I am now sitting in the warm living room of Sandy's house, where I will most likely stay for the next few days.

Things have happened so quickly and my surroundings have changed so abruptly that I cannot separate one sensation from another. And now as the grandfather clock on the wall booms out 12:20 AM, I'll crawl in with a very tired and overflowing head.

Skip | SEPTEMBER 25, BAKER LAKE

In spite of my late bed time last night, I was unable to sleep past 6:30 AM and so now while Sandy and Jim sleep in nearby rooms, I sit in a living room and enjoy for the first time in a long time the comfort, warmth and security of a house on a rainy day. I can simply stare out the window at the scattered rain and the quiet cold of the morning and feel wonderfully warm and happy, part of this precious feeling of return.

PM. Following an excellent bacon-and-egg breakfast with Sandy and Jim, I attended the Anglican Sunday service . . . all in Eskimo, except for one prayer and a hymn solo by Canon James, perhaps for my benefit.

The church is small, white frame with green trim; sound-board interior and rubbed oak furnishings make a clean, bright atmosphere for the intensity and purity of this mass. Eskimo waited outside until the Parson arrived and then filed in, each one carefully wiping his rubber or sealskin boots at the door; men and older children on the left; women and babies on the right. Dress varied from the caribou clothing of a few youngsters to the ill-fitting double-breasted serge coat of the organist. The women all wore berets of bright colors, skirts of solid greens and reds with embroidered border strips and duffel parkas, some with extra hoods to carry their babies. The men wore similar parkas, wool trousers and rubber boots. Children were very well-behaved and sang with terrific volume and fair unison . . . adult singing generally amounted to wailing grunts.

Back to Sandy's after the service for a light lunch and a snooze; then over to the store for a chocolate bar, sealskin boots (dry feet at last), wolf skin for home and mittens.

Jim and I are becoming good friends and took a long hike together to Cemetery Hill overlooking the settlement and then spent an enjoyable hour in the evening talking of hunting, barrens, Iglootik, and the HBC for young men; home to dinner of caribou hash, great stuff, and then a fine evening of maps, books and stories of the North.

Once again I feel the stirrings of intrigue and curiosity in my mind as I learn more and more about the Arctic. Earlier, at Ft. Albany with Art,

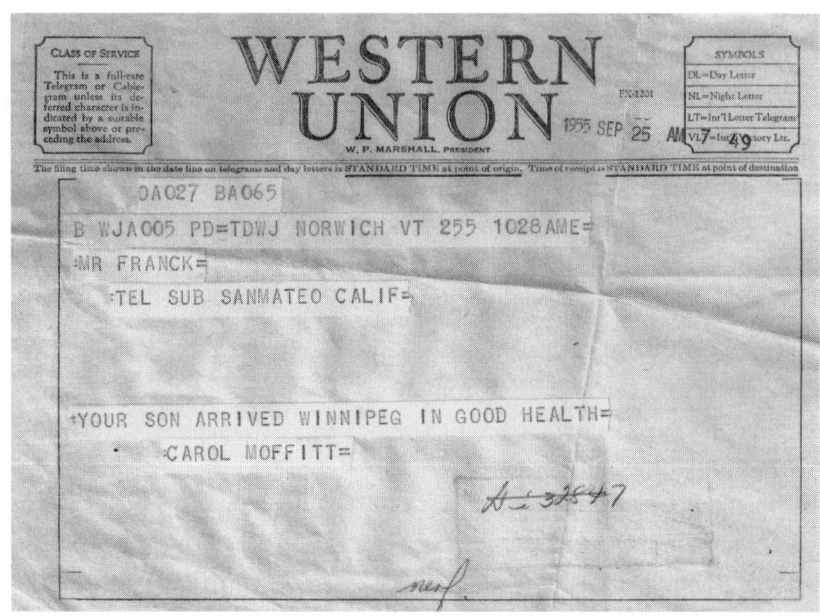

CLASS OF SERVICE
This is a full-rate Telegram or Cablegram unless its deferred character is indicated by a suitable symbol above or preceding the address.

WESTERN UNION
W. P. MARSHALL, PRESIDENT

SYMBOLS
DL=Day Letter
NL=Night Letter
LT=Int'l Letter Telegram
VLT=Int'l Victory Ltr.

FX-1201

1955 SEP 25 AM 7 49

The filing time shown in the date line on telegrams and day letters is STANDARD TIME at point of origin. Time of receipt is STANDARD TIME at point of destination

DA027 BA065
B WJA005 PD=TDWJ NORWICH VT 255 1028AME=
=MR FRANCK=
=TEL SUB SANMATEO CALIF=

=YOUR SON ARRIVED WINNIPEG IN GOOD HEALTH=
=CAROL MOFFITT=

Telegram sent from Carol Moffatt to Thomas Franck, Peter Franck's father, on September 25. Courtesy Fay Franck.

it sparked, only to smolder in the intervening years. Sometime soon I must come back, farther north, in the winter.

Carol's message to have Art buried here at Baker Lake eliminates a lot of expense and worry for the present, and I think it is absolutely appropriate. I would choose exactly that if it had been me instead of Art. I'll arrange with Canon James in the morning, clear legalities with Corporal Dent and arrange for plane; tonight, one more chocolate bar and to bed.

Skip | SEPTEMBER 26, BAKER LAKE

The morning was depressing, but necessary, with Cpl. Dent completing police records of the accident, Art's death, and checking over the customs papers.

Lunch with Sandy and his famous caribou soup . . . top drawer! A whole hind leg boiled for two days with all kinds of semi-secret ingredients added.

And then a fine pick-me-up conversation with Father Rio over a bottle of home brew wine. The Father is a regular guy; long gray beard, intense blue eyes set deep in his wrinkled, brown face, topped with a battered black beret. He is from the apple region of Brittany and we spent most of the time talking about relative merits of ciders and wines; finally decided on a dried raisin wine. He is a very energetic, dynamic man who still looks forward to many years of travel with the Eskimo; seems to know them well and is extremely tolerant of the problems of clashing cultures; supper of caribou steak and rice pudding.

Hope to arrange for a charter flight to the cache tomorrow afternoon so will spend tomorrow morning building a coffin out of packing crate wood.

The days are wonderful adventures of fascinating events and new people. As I write this in the evening, I am resentful of sleep and impatient for the new day to begin.

Skip | SEPTEMBER 27, BAKER LAKE

I spent all morning and most of the afternoon with two Eskimo, Nago and Louie Tapita, constructing a sturdy coffin out of scrap lumber from the weather station. It took a while to get the idea and dimensions across to them; Nago speaks no English and Louie only a bit, but once we understood each other, I soon became a spectator to the operation. Care, ingenuity and pride of craftsmanship combined to produce a fine job.

With the completed box piled on a large dog sledge, Nago and I perched on top, we began a noisy and closely observed procession from the east end of the settlement to the HBC shed at the west end, where we stored our cargo to await its somber destiny.

Checked in with Canon James to report on the coffin construction; endured gossip of Churchill, tea and the officers' wives, and the relative merits of Spic and Span, for the pleasure of tea with lots of sugar, bread (with much raving) and the last remnants of a famous fruitcake.

Scurried home to Sandy's in order to make the 5 PM deadline for a fine dinner of ptarmigan breasts and boiled potatoes.

After a good meal (but still one in which the necessary manners of a guest refuse the release to satisfaction), I spent the evening with Father

Rio and his excellent raisin wine. The Father is really a charming person, still alive and interested in the country and travel. He has many personal stories of his early days in the North, all of which reflect insight and understanding. Maps, music, biscuits and stories of the old North passed the time quickly until 9:30 PM hustled me back to Sandy's for tea before 10 o'clock bedtime.

I still find it impossible to pass up an invitation which offers the possibility of food, and I admit that my afternoon hikes often revolve around good "hand out houses."

Skip | SEPTEMBER 28, BAKER LAKE

Morning rain and heavy overcast ruled out any possibility of the plane arriving from Churchill today for a trip to Marjorie Lake.

Morning spent reading, sorting the "smelly" from the not so "smelly," and reveling in the luxury of watching the rain change to snow and blow on the north wind from behind the warmth of a window pane.

Lunch of "bottom of the pot" caribou soup and my first taste of a local version of bannock . . . tops!; terminated by Sandy's "Have some more tea?" "No." "Good, let's sit."

Took an afternoon walk into the nearby hills; passed a tent camp on the shore of a small pond; watched a woman catching whitefish with a gig line . . . squeals with every catch. As I walked, a man appeared behind his team of six dogs and *kamotik* loaded with caribou skins. He was traveling slowly over bare ground, so I was able to follow him back to the store, where I witnessed my first real trading scene. Sandy presiding in a friendly and masterful way, counting the pelts as Nago, his helper, unpacked them from the caribou bag bundles. When they were counted, Sandy called the total to the Eskimo who nodded in a rather subdued manner. Then from the fur room Sandy leads the procession into the store room for the second part of the transaction. The price of the skins is counted out on the counter in aluminum discs which denote $1.00, $.50, $.25, etc. Sandy then asks the man what he wants to buy and after each purchase, takes the price of the article away from the pile of discs. This continues until the discs are gone. In this case, the man first bought tea, cartridges and sugar; matches followed, and then a succession of small items each of which took long deliberation and evoked much laughter and fun; ribbon, beret, towel, toothpaste (insisting on Colgate) and chewing gum. After the transaction was completed, Sandy invites the man into his kitchen for a cup of tea and then sees the fellow off on his return, everyone smiling.

Perhaps this was not a typical scene in as much as most of the natives are off hunting and the store is not at all busy; however, in spite of Sandy's obvious direction of the entire deal and the complete dependency of the Eskimo on the fairness of the trader, everything seems to have run smoothly and to everyone's satisfaction.

11 PM; Sandy went to bed an hour ago, and as I sit here writing, the snow which started earlier in the evening continues to fall, already covering the ground with a thin blanket of whiteness. It looks bad for a plane tomorrow and the prospects of leaving this country before freeze up becomes less and less. Perhaps I will see my Arctic winter sooner than expected.

Skip | SEPTEMBER 29, BAKER LAKE

I woke up this morning to a dazzling white landscape. About ½ inch of snow had fallen during the night and although it had stopped by daylight, the freezing weather (24F) retained the snow all day. As I looked out the window my mind wandered back to Sept. 9 when we experienced our first blizzard on the Dubawnt and how it had numbed and shocked us so badly.

From the security of shelter, warmth and food, the coming of winter is an interesting, often pleasant and exciting time; but not when we were exposed, hungry and wet.

After the long summer of constant physical activity, the ease and relative inactivity of the past few days, although very welcome at first, is now becoming burdensome. The post has been pretty well explored, and although there are plenty of interesting people to talk to, my body is in serious need of exercise. Sandy refuses to let me work at the post; "Against Co. rules." So I hope to find work somewhere else; outdoors if possible.

And now as the possibility of a plane fades, the matter of support presents a problem. I can't continue living free off the Co. and cannot afford to pay for room and board! Dish washing or cooking for the DOT looms as a possible opportunity. Seeing the winter in the North may cost a bit of a price.

Skip | SEPTEMBER 30, BAKER LAKE

Winds, cold weather and occasional snow flurries continue in the first real approach of steady winter weather. Everyone hopes for one more warm spell before "freeze up," but the old-timers shake their heads doubtfully and insist, "She's closin' down for good."

I was able to get a little exercise this morning helping Jim and Nago move three small skiffs into winter storage and then finished off the morning carrying canned soft drinks from the store to the attic storage in Sandy's house.

In order to conserve fuel and also to discourage the natives from lingering in the store during cold winter days, the Co. insists that no heat whatsoever be used in the store itself; so all goods that would be damaged by freezing must be moved into warmer storage. Sandy and Jim conduct the winter trading dressed in their caribou skins and only open the store for a few hours at a time when the traders congregate at the door. An ice archway is built around the door early in the winter and this, combined with the snowbanks built up against each wall, serve to protect the entrance from the increasing winter winds. Nevertheless, the trading is generally done under freezing conditions, much to the discomfort of bare hands and numb feet. Every aspect of the dealing is conducted with utmost speed, even handling the discs and the grading of furs is designed to speed up the trade. Buy, sell, and then quickly out of the store and back into the warm house.

More wires from interested magazines in the States and Canada. I had no idea our jaunt was causing such a stir, even without the morbid attraction of the accident; wish Art could be here to benefit from his long years of preparation and finally begin to realize the potential of all his hopes and plans. It is difficult to know just how far to go with the news coverage of the recovery and burial story, but perhaps the financial assistance for Carol would make it all worthwhile.

Within the past week I have been exposed to a bit more of the publicity-publication game and from the looks of things there are many possibilities to turn wilderness travel into reasonable revenue. Photography may be a key to the pressing dilemma of life vs. livelihood, which is so often on my mind.

Early afternoon, after enjoying a delightful luncheon of "pancake Friday" with Jim and Sandy, was spent trading telegrams with Life and Colliers and two to Carol and home.

Got in on the last stages of removing the engine from an old rotten boat and on the way back was able to approach Irwin Williams, the officer in charge at DOT, about working for my grub at his station. At first things didn't seem very promising, but after a bit of conversation, it was decided that I could move in with two bachelor boys, Eric and Hillyard. So after a last supper of excellent caribou steaks and boiled potatoes with Sandy, I packed my belongings and "portaged" to the DOT shacks at the other end of the settlement.

A stag party was in progress when Jim and I arrived and so I was able to meet the entire collection of single guys at Baker Lake and share a fine batch of "home made" brew. They are from many regions of Canada and the Commonwealth; connected either with DOT or the MET, or as carpenters and other tradesmen. And all, with the exception of Jim, are in the North for one expressed purpose . . . to make money as fast as possible and then return to the outside. No attempt seems to be made by them to learn about the land or the people; new ways are adopted as little as possible. They cling to the manner of life on the Outside with ridiculous tenacity, often preferring downright discomfort and dissatisfaction to the "dirty native way." Cold, damp feet; blazing hot oil burners and continual colds seem preferred to caribou clothing and a bit of healthy outdoor activity. So here I am, having left the punctual regularity and excellent cooking of Sandy's HBC kingdom, smack in the middle of erratic, restless bachelor quarters surrounded by a mountain of canned goods and home brew. But it is better to at least appear to be self-supporting. I am definitely more independent and probably will be able to eat more; but the charm of the HBC itself; Sandy's personality with his intriguing familiarity with the "old" days and the closer contact with the Eskimo will be missed. I will have to watch carefully so I don't fall into the obvious rut of sleep, eat, drink and grow soft.

Skip | OCTOBER 1, BAKER LAKE

The effects of last night's "home brew" session must have laid the DOT guys pretty low; not a soul appeared until 10 o'clock. Recollections of the evening's escapades mingled with moans of "What a batch!"

Most of the day was spent reading and chatting with these guys. Hillyard, in particular, is a very interesting guy, especially his accounts of Antarctica. One soon gets used to his British air of unconscious conceit and superiority.

A canoe trip through the Back River country looms as a most intriguing possibility, country and people perhaps the most primitive in Canada.

Dinner with the Streets was a pleasant affair, but as yet my unreasonable appetite makes visiting a rather strained situation; all that food sitting on the table and " . . . No thank you, I've had plenty."

Biggest find was a beautiful recording of the complete *La Boheme* in Hillyard's collection. It almost smokes with my use; visions of home, fireplace, Mom and Dad, mingle with the beautiful music in a misty consciousness of far-off desires. Dana too breaks into this atmosphere of return, with misgivings of an uncertain relationship. The bustle and priorities of college life seem far off indeed.

Skip | OCTOBER 2, BAKER LAKE

Cold weather continues and until I receive my duffel parka from Ecomilak, I am pretty well limited to short walks near the post. Hope to be able to pack into the surrounding country for a few days at a time later on and there also might be a chance to tag along on a late caribou hunt, or later when the traps are set out. Have to keep moving or the huge quantity of food that I eat and the soft lethargy of the post will really ruin me.

After dinner with the Stelks, followed by a rather trying round of Hearts, I returned to the DOT to find a new couple playing pool with Ray, Eunice and Ernie. We were soon curled around a bottle of scotch, enjoying a real intellectual spark. They have both studied at U. of Toronto and are quite interested in anthropology. Eunice is a rather sophisticated lady with a great sense of humor. Ernie, much more practical, is a fine guy, living in the Arctic because he likes the country, appreciates the isolation and is profoundly interested in the fate of the natives and the future of the North. He contrasts sharply with the money-making gripers among the other whites of the settlement. Night passed and we were still talking as the sun rose in the first calm, clear sky I have seen since arriving at Baker. Hope to continue our conversations at Ernie's place tomorrow evening with the added attraction of Father Rio and his wine.

Skip | OCTOBER 6, BAKER LAKE

Days of full stomach, late hours, occasional work (dish washing, oil drums) and complete lack of sustained exercise pass in a very lethargic manner, relieved at times by interesting talks with Father Rio, Sandy, the Saunders, and short walks after ptarmigan and fresh air; until the arrival of an RCMP Peterhead from Chesterfield.

Then, as often is the case, when things begin to happen, they develop at a furious rate. Yesterday evening, while attending a "slide session" at Clair's, speculation and the uncertain possibility to catch a ride on the RCMP boat to Chesterfield jelled into a definite "leave right after dinner tomorrow; plenty of room if you are ready." Ed Boone, the Mounty skipper and a prototype of the traditional, rugged RCMP Mounty, also seemed to like my chances of transportation from Chesterfield to Churchill, either on the HBC's Fort Severn due at Chesterfield on its return from Igwalik, or on one of the occasional "cancel flights" connected with Dew Line transportation, or possibly on the Peterhead itself, if the weather holds fair.

So back to the bachelor quarters I went with my head full of the many necessary preparations before departing; packing, arranging for burial, recovery of equipment and film; goodbyes, and seemingly hundreds of odds and ends.

And now as the time to leave the settlement is close at hand, I feel a genuine sadness at saying goodbye to a group of fine people who were extremely kind and hospitable to a young, grubby American. The hope of seeing an Arctic winter first hand is by no means dead; only postponed in favor of a strong desire for home.

CHESTERFIELD

October 7–October 10

Skip | OCTOBER 7, ON BOARD THE PETERHEAD

Up at 7 AM after a 2 AM night before; weary eyes give way to the pressure of finishing up the business of leaving before the Peterhead pulls out. Sandy, Canon James and Clair all combine to take care of details of remains and equipment. Canon James says goodbye with a rather pointed sermon on Christian strength and comfort in the assurance of this transitory life of ours . . . edging toward the door as quickly as possible. Last drink of hot rum with Sandy and Jim; tents and equipment nailed in wooden box, personal belongings jammed into a pack; inadequate goodbyes to my friends, and then into the canoe and out to an impatient Peterhead crew. A few moments later, the diesel is rumbling; the anchor splashes free, and standing on the stern deck, I can watch Baker Lake post gradually disappear behind the tossing winter sea.

Looking around me, I see a very striking fellow at the helm; tall, dark and decidedly handsome, his appearance combining features of both Eskimo and white man. This is Itinewa, a special constable at Chesterfield RCMP and son of Peter Freuchen, the renowned Danish arctic explorer and traveler. The rest of the crew, besides Boone, consists of two Eskimos: Jasper, short, long stringy hair, popping eyes; and Aliak, young, bushy hair with a permanent smile and flashing eyes. An Eskimo couple and their young daughter complete our human cargo.

Shortly after leaving the settlement, we put the tender ashore at two points along the coast and picked up six caribou that the crew had gotten the day before. The carcasses and pelts were piled on the deck just forward of the mast, conveniently located aft of the galley door. Just before lunch and dinner, our steward, Jasper, neatly chops a few chunks off the nearest carcass and we are soon enjoying boiled "tuktu," strictly fresh.

Just before dusk, we entered a narrow bay with high rock shores; anchored for the night and took the young girl ashore to a nearby Eskimo camp where she will stay until her mother returns from the hospital in Chesterfield. We sleep in very low-ceilinged bunks (about 18" from mattress to ceiling) right next to the engine, two bunks on each side. Warm and stuffy, but nevertheless most welcome after a windy, cold day on deck with icy spray flying.

Skip | OCTOBER 8, ON BOARD THE PETERHEAD

Our morning start was delayed due to fog and a fruitless caribou hunt. After the fog lifted, we proceeded down the lake, stopping occasionally to look for caribou sign; no luck. Made anchor in another small bay after lunch, and while Itinewa and the young chaps went out for caribou, Ed and I took a hike in the opposite direction. We saw a lot of sign, but nothing moving; total bag one lone ptarmigan. Just as we returned to the boat, two shots rang out down the bay and Jasper prančed around the deck waving his arms and shouting, "tuktu, tuktu!" So I guess we'll have plenty of meat for the rest of the trip. Ed went out to meet the men and help bring the meat out to the boat. I stayed on board, cleaned the ptarmigan and began preparing a stew; heavy on the potatoes with only one ptarmigan.

Skip | OCTOBER 9, ON BOARD THE PETERHEAD

Returned about 10 miles along the shore of Baker Lake to drop Sukpa's wife at the camp where the little girl was left yesterday. Radio message from Baker informed us that we had the wrong woman aboard; what a system!

Somehow, Dent got the wrong family and did not find the error until after we had left. She, apparently, did not dare question the RCMP authority and so was going for an unknown ride with no comment. Her husband continues with us to Chesterfield and the hospital.

Weather is cold, but with only a slight breeze blowing, we can stay on deck for a while before diving below for a hot cup of tea.

As we left Baker Lake and entered the narrows at the western end of Chesterfield Inlet, we saw quite a bit of game on the nearby stony ridges which follow close along the shore. Wolf, fox, "tuktu," rabbit, ptarmigan, all in their winter coats, stand out plainly against the dark rock and brown moss. The lack of snow certainly betrays the Arctic animals early in this season, especially the ptarmigan; they huddle among the rocks in assumed safety and actually are more easily seen at a great distance. They seem to play the role of the porcupine in the bush to the south; a starving man could easily keep himself going by killing these slow birds with a stick or a stone; handy things to have around. The Peterhead is just about the ideal boat for arctic waters. She is about 45' with 12.5' beam; plenty of freeboard, and square stern and a stubby, heavy bow. The hold can accommodate about 14T and is situated right amidships with the engine room and forecastle aft and the galley forward. She is gaff rigged and although I have never seen the sails set, they seem to be adequate for emergency use. It would be a simple matter to convert such a ship to pleasure use by sacrificing part of the hold for a main cabin which would provide standing room with very little cabin structure above deck. The aft forecastle could then be used for storage and additional bunks. The hull is made of sturdy oak planking capable of working in drift ice and stout enough to allow for grounding on a soft bottom. The foresails seem inadequate for any efficient sailing and are probably the key to conversion to sail. The running rigging also would have to be lightened considerably before she would perform smartly. But all in all, the Peterhead has many fine qualities and offers a starting prototype toward that mythical dream ship of mine.

It's a terrific feeling to travel all day and then as dusk falls, to work along the coast until a suitable bay is sighted, then silently slip into a calm, snug anchorage, drop the hook and start the pot boiling; a dry, comfortable home wherever you are. A perfect way to combine home and adventure, if the proper folks are part of the home and the adventure.

Wind shifted to the east and brought with it colder temperatures and a heavy snow storm. The snow still melts on the moving ship so that the only effect is driving snow in my face, clothes a little wetter than usual, and a very slippery deck for sealskin boots. However, my curious habit of becoming cook wherever I go results in a fair amount of time in the warm galley.

Tonight as the anchor runs out, I am putting the finishing touches on a sturdy ptarmigan-tuktu stew complete with pots, onion, turnips, beans and corn, all from cans, of course, but . . . ; tea and hardtack complete the banquet. Itinewa and Aliak eat their meals quickly and finish off with an encouraging, "kabloonak, good!"

Skip | OCTOBER 10, ON BOARD THE PETERHEAD

The snow of last evening pretty well disappeared by the time we crawled out into the cold, pre-dawn darkness this morning. All of us congregated in the galley, six cramped and somewhat ripe men, while the trusty primus sputtered its warmth into our space and the precious tea pot. Breakfast of tea, bread and honey followed by a smoke and then when the sun rose high enough to furnish enough light so that Itinewa could pick his course through the islands of the inlet, engines roared, anchor hauled and off we went. The wind was raw and the sea was breaking just aft of our beam, but the combination of my duffel parka and an occasional two-step shuffle kept me fairly warm.

The distant ridges along both shores were sugared in white and presented an impressive contrast with the black, icy water of the inlet. After an hour or so of running, the rest of the crew went below for a warming "mug up," leaving Aliak at the wheel and me as silent company. Standing on the stern deck, I had a fine view of the tumbling sea around us and soon caught sight of my first seal. The dark, smooth head with long bristling mustache rose almost erect in the water, closely resembling a man looking around with just his head above water. This particular fellow seemed all alone and after giving us a quick once over, disappeared into the waves. Interesting, but can't say I envy him his cold, wet habitat.

Itinewa returned to relieve us and Aliak and I are now enjoying the warmth and tea of the galley. Writing serves as a fine excuse for remaining below a little longer; these ship-board entries are perhaps a little longer than usual.

Sukpa, the tubercular Eskimo, sits across from me silently sucking on his pipe. Long, stringy, gray-black hair hangs down to his shoulders, framing a wrinkled brown face with blue, obedient eyes. Brown, well-worn teeth show in his occasional smile and otherwise are clinched viselike around the mended stem of his old pipe.

The jib is set now to ease the heavy pitching of the boat in a short chop. Even this old, rust-stained foresail looks good and seems to dress up the boat a little. "Chesterfield by 1 PM" is the cry; snowing again; wet, heavy flakes.

"Winter time not so good for boat! Komatik better!"

10 AM. Driving snow covers everything. Visibility very poor, but Itinewa's instinct keeps a steady course.

Epilogue

Members of the Moffatt Party in Churchill, Manitoba, after arriving Baker Lake, Nunavut on September 24, 1955. From left: George Grinnell, Bruce LeFavour, Joe Lanouette, and Peter Franck. Courtesy Fay Franck.

GRINNELL'S ACCOUNT of the Moffatt Dubawnt journey was generally well-received by reviewers and the wilderness canoeing community and generated considerable comment and criticism, mostly negative, about Art Moffatt as leader of the journey and about the journey itself, its organization, provisions, travel style, group dynamics, and the fatal accident. His account is a well-written, sometimes poetic, personal reminiscence of his Dubawnt trip. But his interpretations of Moffatt's state of mind and motives to lead the 1955 adventure lack convincing evidence and seem more directed at trying to understand and explain Grinnell's own tragic life and personal struggle against a patrician heritage.

Andrew Macdonald writes in his review of *A Death on the Barrens*, "After wrestling with this for some time I concluded what this book is not. The book is not a journal, it is not a trip report, it is not an autobiography, and most importantly, it is not just a true story."[1] So this memoir is my attempt to fill that gap and perhaps add objectivity to the historical record of the Moffatt party. It is indeed a "journal" and a "trip report," providing a daily, chronologic account, from my twenty-two-year-old perspective. I have included excerpts from Peter Franck's Dubawnt journal with my own entries for the same date, providing, I hope, a broader perspective on daily events and greater insights into individual personalities.

Response to Grinnell's account of the Moffatt journey was considerable, ranging from Bob Thum's arrogant remarks that "those guys had no business being up there. . . . They fooled around and did a lot of crap"[2] and James Murphey's description, "an excellent example of how not to conduct a canoe trip"[3] to Stewart Coffin's evaluation that "the Moffatt Expedition stands as the pioneering venture in modern recreational canoe travel through the subarctic tundra of northern Canada."[4]

So where did it go wrong?

I don't think our food supplies were significantly compromised by the failure of our original order to arrive on schedule at Stony Rapids. Variety may have suffered and greater reliance on canned goods available at Stony probably increased the total weight of the supplies and thereby burdened our portage loads, but not to a critical degree. Our standard daily meals were generally minimal, approximately 2,400 calories[5] for an oatmeal breakfast with milk and sugar, lunch of pilot biscuit, cheese, jam, and peanut butter, and a glop[6] dinner. This basic menu was frequently, but not regularly, augmented by instant pudding dessert, berries with milk, a johnny cake treat, mushrooms, chocolate, caribou organs and meat, ptarmigan, fish, and roe. But even with these additions we were probably well short of the recommended 4,000 calories per day.[7]

Two aspects of our food supplies and trip diet did impact our group dynamics and energies. The sugar shortage was, I think, more a matter of self-discipline (or the lack thereof) than a serious health or energy issue. It did, however, contribute significantly to tension and group conflict. The lack of fat in our diet, on the other hand, probably contributed to a serious caloric deficiency that may have exacerbated our discomfort in the cold, wet late season and may have resulted in reduced energy and endurance. We made a curious mistake early in the trip in not taking advantage of the Canada goose as a ready source of fat, as Tom Bose reports,[8] although perhaps the need for animal fat in our diet was not as apparent when the birds were readily available and wood for roasting fires was also on hand. Cooking a sturdy goose on a smoldering heather/twig fire on a wet, windy day in the Barrens would probably have been a real challenge, no matter how much we craved the fat.

In terms of generally available canoeing and camping equipment that we might have lacked and which therefore might have contributed to our delayed travel schedule, George Luste, in his thoughtful commentary on the Moffatt journey,[9] notes that a spray cover over at least the canoe bow might have facilitated running some rapids without shipping water. I think that is true. Similarly, a snap-on cover over the midship canoe load would not only have protected against waves lapping over the gunnels but also, perhaps more importantly, would have made travel during moderate rain/wind conditions more likely, protecting supplies and equipment while promoting canoe miles during marginal weather conditions.

Our tents were classic World War II two-man mountain tents that were still, even fifteen years after their development, probably the best available at the time. But it is important to note that in those early years of canoeing and trip planning in the '50s, neither Art nor I were informed, nor particularly interested in, what technical advances in expedition equipment or canoeing technology might have already existed or might have been under way. Indeed, our philosophical minimalist approach to wilderness travel probably was a deterrent to thinking about such things as homemade spray covers.

So if nutritional deficiencies and the lack of improved equipment technologies did not doom the Moffatt Dubawnt journey, what were the fatal flaws?

Grinnell suggests two sources that contributed to the tragic death of Art Moffatt. I disagree emphatically with both.

The suggestion that Art was suicidal and indifferent to the well-being of other party members (something of a Hornby cliché) has been expressed by some reviewers and correspondents within the wilderness canoeing community.[10] This assumption of Art's mental instability, I believe, derives from Grinnell's brief description of Art's reaction to his broken tea cup: "With his broken tea cup lying shattered at his feet, Art became convinced that he would never see his wife and children again, and so he sat, and so we waited."[11] I know of no evidence in support of this analysis of Art's mental condition. How did Grinnell get into Art's mind to know what Art was "convinced" of? Actually, Art considered the incident of the broken tea cup as "an omen of bad luck" (journal entry, June 21),[12] not as a moment of fatal abandonment.

Grinnell's account of the dream sequence that Art described in his journal entry of September 2—"and in the clear water below, I could see a gray canoe (mine?) broken and resting on the bottom among caribou bones"—ends with a positive statement: "Must get out of here soon, and will."[13] But that statement was not part of the dream. It was written the following day, September 3, expressing concern about the cold and another nontravel day, clearly a positive commitment in the face of deteriorating weather and in spite of the adverse imagery of the previous night's dream.

Grinnell mentions another dream attributed to Art for which I have no evidence: "Art dreamed that there was a toll at the end of the lake which he could not afford to pay."[14] There is no mention of this "dream" in Art's journal.

Commenting on Art's need for money to feed his family, Grinnell continues to fuel his "suicidal" theory by glibly stating that before the Dubawnt trip, Art had three choices: he could take a job in New York, "or he could double his life insurance and buy a one-way ticket to the Great Beyond; or he could gamble on a wildlife film. He chose the last two."[15]

Many people increase life insurance coverage anticipating some special travel or experience. The presence of insurance policy kiosks at major airports suggests that this is a fairly common transaction. I have no evidence that Art did, indeed, increase his life insurance coverage prior to the Dubawnt trip, but if he did, it might better be interpreted as an act of family responsibility rather than some suicidal impulse.

Early in his narrative, Grinnell describes the group's frustration while wind-bound on July 2 at Black Lake and quotes Art: "'I felt sad, apprehensive, and gloomy . . .' Art wrote on the eve of our adventure."[16] Actually that quote was from Art's journal entry for June 16, 4:20 p.m. at White

River Junction, Vermont, in which he describes his feelings as he stands on the station platform, saying goodbye to his wife, Carol, and waiting for the train to take him, Joe, Bruce, and Peter to Montreal and then westward to Toronto, Sioux Lookout, and Prince Albert, Saskatchewan. The complete quote ended with "and my immediate worry was the film." This refers to the fact that earlier in the day the unexposed 16 mm movie film supply was not ready at a local camera shop and Art was concerned about the delayed delivery of the missing film. I joined the party in Toronto. George Grinnell did not join the party until June 27 in Stony Rapids. The quote had nothing to do with our situation at Black Lake.

Art had a loving wife and two lovely daughters at home. He had his journal and film growing in detail and complexity of the trip account, the raw materials in support of his professional breakout as a wilderness adventurer and journalist. He was a quietly principled man who from an early age lived as best he could, consistent with his principles. He had a small inheritance that offered a bit of flexibility in lifestyle choices but was by no means a maintenance income. He was a pacifist and volunteered for the American Field Service as an ambulance driver, serving in Africa and Italy during World War II. He was a college graduate in geology and literature, worked as editor of *Ski* magazine, and developed a seasonal business leading young teenagers on summer canoe trips down the Albany River. He had canoed that same river solo in 1928 and with his wife, Carol, in 1948. He projected those Albany River experiences to the grand concept of retracing J. B. Tyrrell's epic 1893 journey down the Dubawnt River, creating a film documentary about the journey and sharing that experience in print and on screen with the wilderness adventure community. Nothing suicidal about that!

Similarly, Peter Franck mentions in his July 23 journal entry a conversation in which he and Art discussed Art's plan for an outdoor film project in the Sierra two years after the Dubawnt project; this is not the typical planning by someone contemplating suicide.

Numerous entries in Art's journal refute Grinnell's interpretation that Art was suicidal and "convinced that he would never see his wife and children again."[17]

August 12: "Cold too, now, but I love these evenings alone by the fire, later at night and early in the morning I smoke, drink tea, think of home, Carol, Creigh, Debbo . . . of my new study and of the children there with me when I get back, and the stories I'll be able to tell them about all my adventures in the North . . . shooting rapids and the time I saw the wolves, white ones, and the caribou and moose and fish and birds."

Sept. 4: "Toward the beginning of the last ½ of the 2½-mi. portage, you leave the hard clay, damp places and come out on an old beach . . . the high point of Hudson Bay's post-glacial submergence: Tyrrell. On this loose gravel were bear tracks and bear turds full of bear berry, and some handsome green and white pebbles, some of which I collected for my girls."

On the end pages of his journal book Art compiled a to-do list of plans and chores upon his return: "Wire Carol from Churchill or Winnipeg, probably Winnipeg, after seeing Wilson of the Beaver. Sell him an article or two, plus a cover and talk to him about film. Ask Carol to come to Mount Royal, Windsor or Laurentides . . . get reservations, bring me clothes. Have a long weekend up there. . . . If I get Toronto in a.m., can see Star during day; if late, see him that p.m. or next a.m. Catch first train from there for Montreal. . . . On return from Bush, see John Coleman, CNR public relations, Montreal, PQ; suggest press conference. Get him to notify Time-Life Bureau, or do it myself."

Clearly, these are not the thoughts of a man who has abandoned hope and does not expect to see his family or associates again.

Grinnell's suggestion that "the movie was not working out: and that . . . Art had not captured on film anything that would pay enough to feed his family"[18] is curious and seriously misunderstands the objectives of the film project. Our photographic mission was not to film wildlife in the traditional professional strategy of sitting concealed, waiting for the perfect shot as Grinnell asserts.[19] We were filming a canoe journey along a transect that reflected remarkable changes in the wildlife and natural history of the region. It was the journey that mattered and it was the context of that journey that we were committed to record. As even the most amateur moviemaker knows, exposed raw film footage is just the beginning of the moviemaking process. It is true that we didn't get a shot of a grizzly's ear or some other spectacular wildlife close-up, but to suggest therefore that the film was a failure and thereby contributed to some deadly depression is absurd.

More importantly, the unsupported assertion that Art was consciously "stalling"[20] so that he could chance on some remarkable wildlife photograph is outrageous. Art and I were transparently committed to filming the entire journey; we were not "waiting for something to photograph."[21] Art was out with the camera whenever he had the opportunity, often in the morning before others were up, or while I was cooking breakfast. And throughout each day, traveling or not, our priority was to get that shot, record that moment, preserve that feeling of being on this amazing adventure. To suggest that Art was stalling is unpardonable.

Before we left the States in June, Art and Carol had recently completed a remodel of their classic New England home. The remodel focused primarily on a new study/workplace with layout benches, photo-editing space, and efficient filing cabinets for research materials, film storage, and manuscript production. The new space smoothly integrated with the traditional architecture of the main house, and Art was very proud of it. He was anxious to return from the Dubawnt journey with as much raw material as possible and then get started in this new space with the professional preparation of his journey accounts.

George Luste writes, perhaps unduly influenced by Grinnell's assertion of the film's inadequacy, "Prospects for his wilderness movie did not look promising, even by September. His stubborn hold on the camera chest during the dump would suggest something akin to that."[22] I suggest that "his stubborn hold" might indicate quite the opposite: that even during those painful, life-threatening, violent moments, Art was attempting to protect and save what was most precious to him; what had the potential to provide the basis for a coherent, artistic expression of this classic journey; and, yes, what perhaps had some potential for financial gain.

I do not believe Art was suicidal. Similarly, I do not believe that he had any significant doubts about the effectiveness of the expedition photography, certainly no concerns that would lead to some sort of dysfunctional depression.

Other aspects of Grinnell's narrative are also troubling and tend to cast doubt on the accuracy of his account.

Peter Franck is characterized as stammering. I cannot recall a single incident in which Peter stammered. Peter's wife, Fay, insists that she never heard Peter stammer, "not even an 'um' or an 'er.'"[23]

Grinnell titles chapter seven "The United Bowman's Association" and discusses at some length the formation of this organization. "After crossing the Height-of-Land, we formed a union and went into revolt."[24] Later in his recollections, he notes, "By the time we bowmen had lost our fear of the wilderness and had taken effective control of the expedition."[25]

Peter makes no mention of the UBA in his journal and only notes, "I am having lots of trouble with George. He just won't do what I tell him and in one bad spot, he refused to do anything and just sat down his paddle" (journal entry, August 6).

I have no recollection of the UBA and did not mention it in my journal, so I wrote Bruce LeFavour, asking him about the UBA. He responded, "The bowman neither individually nor as a group ever contemplated taking over the leadership of the expedition. The very idea is ridiculous. Rather, as I remember it, the name and the extremely loose organization was a joke, a way for us to vent our frustrations with some of Art's actions. . . . The UBA was simply a way for the three of us to bitch among ourselves and thereby relieve some tension, not in any way a revolt."[26]

And yet, in *Canoe* magazine, July 1988, Grinnell wrote, "In the last days of August, now that we were in command, we took more holidays than Moffatt had ever contemplated."[27] I have no idea what he was imagining.

On August 26, I made a very dumb mistake, swamping my canoe while it was close to shore. My journal entry describes the incident: "And the grand booby prize of the trip to Pessl for swamping his canoe while standing up to put on a parka. Damn near tipped the whole works over. Cold hour spent drying slightly damp hardtack and very wet Skip after having to dive for dishes in about four feet of icy water. Warm sun soon took care of both and we were off again, stopped within an hour due to high winds and a nearby herd of caribou."

Peter describes the incident: "While Skip was standing up taking a piss out of the canoe, he slipped and fell on the gunnel and the whole works almost went over. He got all wet and the canoe partly filled, but we soon got ashore and dried everything."

But Grinnell describes the accident in much more dramatic, complex, and exaggerated terms. "Skip was furious. He was so angry he slammed the bow of his green canoe full speed onto the rocky bank. Jumping out of his seat, he scrambled forward over the load looking as if he were going to kill Art. Fortunately, he lost his balance and ended up in the water with the contents of his capsized canoe on top of him."[28]

According to Grinnell, my anger derived from an alleged incident earlier in the day when Art's canoe became separated from the others and George and I argued whether we should turn around to search for Art or let him catch up as best he could. "He (Skip) wanted to turn our canoes broadside to the waves and go check on Art. . . . I felt he was, as usual, being unnecessarily paternalistic. I favored continuing on in the direction of the wind and waves and to let Art and Joe catch up to us when and if they desired . . . finally Skip picked up his paddle and swung his green canoe around . . . and after more than an hour struggling broadside to the now dangerous waves, we reached the island. From a cliff we heard Art's voice yell down to us 'Hold it guys, I want to get you coming in on a big one.' The next wave nearly swamped our canoes. We heard Art's camera 'whirr,' and then he said, 'OK. Got it!' Skip's face turned various shades of crimson."[29]

I have no recollection of this incident and neither Peter nor I mention it in the journals. We both describe "swamping" the canoe and "the canoe partly filled." But Grinnell's description dramatically exaggerates: "Fortunately, he lost his balance and ended up in the water with the contents of his capsized canoe on top of him."

Art does not mention the dramatic photo shoot of the canoes "coming in on a big one" as Grinnell describes, but he does narrate the events of August 26, paddling northward on Dubawnt Lake:

> Paddled in lee of island, found huge 4-ft. rollers coming off the lake there, went out in them toward next island but could see that if wind came up hard as it had begun rollers would crest and we'd be in trouble, so rode them a mile toward next big island. Other 2 canoes were cutting more east and got off course, but did not follow me even when I was obviously going elsewhere. Suddenly had to pee very

badly before I could reach lee of point, couldn't make it had to let go in pants . . . mad as hell.

Then Skip came up, mad because I hadn't made clear where I was going . . . more words between us. . . . Then Skip almost upset his canoe putting on parka, got it full of water, had to dump and unload, dive for dropped dishes. Spent hours getting re-organized, then on couple miles, saw 40 Canada Geese, stopped where we saw caribou on island."[30]

September 6, we saw a grizzly as we paddled along the shore of Grant Lake. We beached the canoes, and Art and I grabbed the cameras and stalked the bear. My journal: "Quite a comical pantomime, the bear grazing from bush to bush with the unconcern of complete confidence, and two rather cautious, crouching forms approaching with noses glued to cameras. It was wonderful; we got very close before he saw us and then he merely looked, sat down, 'thought it over,' ambled close to satisfy his curiosity and then making a tremendous picture silhouetted full length against the sky to examine these strange intruders. We played ring around each other for a while until the bear worked down wind of us and within 100' or so. Then instead of running from the human scent, he continued right for us. Rather than be caught with the bear between us and the canoes, Art and I ran for the shore, and this sudden movement was enough to turn the bear and send him scampering over the rocks along the shore and out of sight."

Peter describes the grizzly encounter: "We had gone maybe 1.5 mi. when we saw a barren ground grizzly on the shore. . . . We pulled over right away and Skip and Art got out to get pictures. Before he saw us, he was wandering around in a lazy way feeding on the hillside every now and then. He would sit down on his seat, just like a toy bear, and look around in a most comic way. When he did see Art and Skip, got up right away and started walking over to see what we were. All of a sudden he started running toward us and Art was so nervous he could hardly work the camera. When he got fairly close, stopped and stood up on his hind legs to have a better look at us. He certainly seemed enormous and he probably tried to get downwind of us. The wind was blowing right toward us off the land, because he walked down to the shore and on to a spit of land just below us, about 50 yd. away. Finally something scared him and he took off over the hills at a terrific pace. A man could never keep away from him by running, if he charged. He got out of sight in no time at all."

Art describes this grizzly encounter:

> Then up along NW shore of Grant Lake about 2 miles . . . we were ¼ mile in lead; I saw what seemed to be a large rock on slope ½ mile from lake; paddled on; looked again, saw it moving; looked back, saw Skip and Bruce waving paddles. Then thought for a moment it was musk ox; then saw it was Barren ground grizzly bear. Paddled back to other canoes fast as possible, where could get through shallows to shore; jumped out with cameras, giving still to Skip, and asking him to follow, get stills.
>
> I ran up slope about 100 yds., set up camera on tripod, focused on bear which was coming toward me. When it moved, it ran. It had seen us and twice reared up on hind legs . . . huge critter, about 7 feet tall with beautiful tawny coat, and powerful, rippling run; legs at ankles seemed as big as my thighs.
>
> Bear kept right on at me . . . shot pix, about 30 feet. Then he circled down wind, and when it seemed he must have our scent, i.e., when he reached lake shore due south of us, he started at us again; Skip and I still 100 yds. inland, 3 canoes aground in very shallow water.
>
> Bruce had spoken of grizzly proclivity to charge, so I was getting nervous. As bear came on fast, Skip and I started to run for canoes, but bear then saw us and apparently got our scent for the first time, or understood what smell was. Anyway, he turned tail, went like express train back along shore, across rocky point, scaring up 3 ptarmigan which flushed white as he ran. He slashed across marshy flat up into dwarf birch hillside and up hill as fast as a horse could gallop. Glad to see him go. Skip and I went to see tracks, couldn't find them.

Grinnell offers a much more melodramatic and questionable account: "The bear, seeing Art charge up the hill, turned and charged down the hill towards him." Art is quoted as yelling at the guys waiting in the canoes,

"Don't shoot it! FOR GOD'S SAKE DON'T SHOOT IT!"[31] even though no one in the canoes had even made a move to find their rifles.[32] Grinnell continues, "Art set up his tripod while the bear continued to charge down the hill at him . . . Art began filming. The bear came down on all fours and resumed its charge . . . Eventually, the bear circled around more cautiously to cut off Art's line of retreat to the canoes; then it lost its nerve all together, wheeled about and galloped hell-bent-for-election towards the far horizon."[33]

Given the speed of a grizzly's charge, that bear must have been pretty far off to spend all that time "charging" and still not get to Art. Unfortunately, I think George Luste is correct when he writes, "George Grinnell's description of his (Art's) encounter with the barren ground grizzly will become a mythical legend."[34] Mythical indeed!

Luste also notes that Art did not bring a gun with him, "and I admire him immensely for this. His younger bowmen did bring guns."[35] True, but Art fully supported and advocated carrying guns to hunt game and augment the food supply. In a pretrip correspondence with Art, J. B. Tyrrell advised Art to carry a "high-powered rifle." Art accepted that advice and was a willing partner in hunting for food by killing animals, no matter who was carrying or using the weapons. And none of the Moffatt party had any interest in or intention of killing bears. Our guns were for food. Caribou and ptarmigan were food; bears were not.

The reminiscences of Grinnell's Dubawnt experience, and indeed of his entire tragic life as published in *A Death on the Barrens,* remain uniquely his and have found a place in the literature of wilderness canoeing. But the true legacy of the Moffatt Dubawnt journey deserves the broader perspective of other voices from those that made the same journey at the same time.

The tragedy of September 14 occurred, in my opinion, not because of Art's alleged mental instability or some sort of Zen nonsense, but because Art and I failed to accurately translate our collective Albany River experiences to northern big-river systems, especially into late-season, freezing conditions, and because we tried to concurrently accomplish two mutually exclusive objectives: travel and film. We succumbed to the romantic notion that we could retrace Tyrrell's epic journey in his image, with hunting-supported food supplies, with traditional, minimalist equipment, without local guides, and at the same time make a movie of it all. Our journey was delayed and tragically interrupted because we did not differentiate between what worked on the Albany River and what would not work in late season on the Dubawnt.

The deteriorating weather exacerbated our concerns about our dwindling food supply, threatening frostbite and unknown downstream river conditions, and it changed our modus operandi from cautious land-based scouting of rapids to a floating assessment as we were sucked into the headwater Vs of each successive rapid. It worked for several days and many rapids, except for one.

So what is the lesson to be learned from the Moffatt Dubawnt experience? Or should there be one? We did not struggle to the Wholdaia Lake height-of-land and then commit to north-flowing Dubawnt waters to teach anyone anything, except ourselves in growing self-knowledge under challenge, awe, and adversity, and perhaps to understand and accept a perspective of our humble humanity within the enormity of nature.

Somewhere between the robotic distance grinds of Thum's "well-oiled machine"[36] and the tragic disregard for time, distance, and season of the Moffatt leadership (and I include myself in that category), there must be a reasonable balance for wilderness canoeists on long journeys that affords safe passage with a flexibility of opportunity, weather, and peripheral interests.

The goal: to avoid a narrow rush from beginning to end and to find "value . . . in the journey itself, in the landscape and one's spiritual relationship with it, the fauna and flora, the solitude and physical joy of paddling"[37]; to arrive at one's destination in good shape, full of a humble sense of profound experience, and maybe a day or two late.

Andrew Macdonald, in his 1996 review of *A Death on the Barrens,* noted that the book was "not just a true story."[38] And indeed the subtitle of the 1996 edition is "a true story." I contend that Grinnell's book is something less than a true story, diminished by outright misrepresentation: Peter Franck was never a stutterer, the United Bowman's Association never took "effective control of the expedition," and Art did not "stall."

The book is further marred by gross melodramatic exaggeration (the grizzly encounter, the "capsized" canoe incident) and out of context, inaccurate quotations (Black Lake, the sunken canoe dream).

Grinnell's account is a distorted, self-serving reminiscence of a man struggling to understand and justify his own tragic life. It is his Dubawnt story, for sure, but it is not the defining record of that remarkable adventure.

My own Dubawnt journey in the summer of 1955 was the single most formative experience of my life. It redirected my education and subsequent professional career. It helped define a maturing political liberalism that led to a vigorous antiwar activism in the 1960s and '70s, and reinforced a growing spirituality based on Nature and a comfortable sense of my place as an animal within the enormous web of life.

The exclamation "this need not be Failure!" (journal entry, August 25) is the liberating cry of a young man finally throwing off parental pressure to pursue a medical career, as had several preceding paternal generations. I had combined literature and premed majors at Dartmouth following the family plan and had completed preliminary entrance forms at the University of Vermont medical school during the spring of my senior year prior to leaving for the Dubawnt. Time and space in the wilderness, time and space in my own mind, nurtured by the Barrens and my sense of somehow belonging in that vastness, gave insight into a future that was becoming my own. Art's knowledge of geology and his general understanding of the natural sciences helped define my growing awareness that I had a personal and possibly professional place somewhere within the natural science disciplines and that that would be honorable and OK.

Returning from the Dubawnt, I enrolled as a special student in geology at the University of Michigan and earned credits in those prerequisite science subjects that had not been part of my premed curriculum. Admitted to the graduate program in geology in 1957, I earned the MS degree with the completion of a thesis project studying the late glacial history of the Illecillewat Glacier in British Columbia, Canada. Fieldwork for that project involved camping in an isolated, high-alpine environment, and this was the beginning of a professional career as a field geologist that took me to remote wilderness areas in east Greenland, Iceland, and southeast Alaska in addition to northern and southern New England and the Pacific Northwest. I had found a career path as "a means of livelihood without the sacrifice of a way of life in nature and wilderness" (journal entry, August 28).

My years at the University of Michigan were focused on redefining an academic path for my professional future, but it was also a time of growing foreign policy tensions. The Korean War was in the face and future of every senior male college student. I enrolled as a special graduate student at the University of Michigan with the clear understanding that acceptance there would temporarily exempt me from the military draft. That was almost as compelling a reason to go back to school as was my ongoing search for a professional career. It took me many years and new experiences to understand that protection against forced participation in military violence was not the same, nor as justified, as active resistance against that same violence. But it was a beginning.

I am not a pacifist. I lack the deep spiritual and philosophical foundation necessary to support and inspire that absolute belief. But Art's pacifism and his support of international human rights as exemplified by his ambulance service during World War II and his outspoken advocacy of justice for indigenous peoples opened my mind to issues of racism, poverty, and U.S. interventionist foreign policy.

I moved to Boston in 1963 as a new hire with the U.S. Geological Survey and in my spare time became involved with the growing antiwar movement in the Boston-Cambridge area, especially after August 1964, when President Johnson received congressional approval via the contrived Tonkin Gulf Resolution to engage U.S. military forces directly in the Vietnam War.

The American Friends Field Service Committee offices in Cambridge provided training and administrative support as I began volunteering as a draft counselor, helping draft-vulnerable young men develop and execute applications for conscientious objector status as an alternative to active military service. My experience within the antiwar movement included withholding federal tax dollars supporting the U.S. Vietnam War effort; the 1967 march on the Pentagon; local speeches, rallies, and demonstrations against the war and U.S. foreign policy.

A critical understanding of who the most vulnerable and exploited domestic victims of the U.S. Vietnam War policy were occurred for me in the early 1970s. It became apparent that draft counseling was serving a predominantly white, wealthy, college-educated clientele with personal access to legal counsel and financial support, while young, predominantly minority men, drafted and already part of the military but confronted with their spiritual, ethical, and political unwillingness to become part of a killing machine, had very little organized support and were really the most vulnerable, helpless victims. That awareness led me from "draft" counseling to "GI" counseling and to the establishment, funding, and operation of the Common Sense Bookstore in Ayer, Massachusetts, a town outside the gates of Fort Devon, a training facility for U.S. Army Special Forces and NSA surveillance teams.

The bookstore indeed sold books, but it was really a resource front for activist support of dissenting GIs who tried either the legal pathway to attain conscientious objector status as an active soldier, or to obtain AWOL support to desert and find sanctuary in foreign countries. The bookstore provided legal, psychological, medical, and limited financial support for these GI dissenters, maintaining sanctuary contacts, mostly in Toronto and Montreal, to facilitate escape from an immoral, illegal war.

I am proud of those antiwar years and the risks my family took in support of that activism. The example of Art's pacifism and his cryptic campfire rhetoric, questioning bureaucratic nationalism and U.S. interventionist foreign policy, helped define the progressive political person I am today. I am grateful.

I read Albert Schweitzer as a senior at Dartmouth and I think I understood his ethic of "the will to live," "reverence for life," and what must follow from these ideas to "reverence every form of life, seeking so far as possible to refrain from destroying any life regardless of its particular type."[39]

After we killed and butchered our first caribou, I commented on the seeming contradiction between my criticism of the "urban" hunter and my eager participation in our aggressive pursuit of every available animal food source: fish, caribou, grouse, ptarmigan (journal entry, August 5). Indeed, we had become a predatory pack, killing and consuming to live, to survive. We were not wasteful; we never killed more than we could use and we ate or used all practical parts of our caribou kills including the liver, heart, and tongue as delicacies, the hide as a lap robe and sleeping pad, and the brains as part of our "tanning" process to soften and preserve the hide.

Schweitzer helped me understand the turmoil I felt between joy and awe while quietly and peacefully walking or paddling among the caribou and the hot, aggressive lust of stalking and waiting for a kill. Then and in subsequent years Schweitzer embraced and explained that contradiction for me.

"[A] person is constantly forced to preserve his own life and life in general only at the cost of other life. If he has been touched by the ethic of reverence for life, he injures and destroys life only under a necessity he cannot avoid and never from thoughtlessness. . . .

"The important thing is that we are part of life. We are born of other lives."[40]

And I am comfortable now accepting that distant predatory role in my life, perhaps recognizing that the bond we felt with the Dubawnt caribou, our dependency and grateful sustenance, was indeed a vehicle, a channel to the profound sense of kinship and intimacy that I now feel for all things wild.

Sitting at the base of an ancient lodgepole pine in present-day southwestern Montana, watching and listening to the clacking of the horns of contending bull elk during the autumn rut is a privileged moment, permitted and ignored by them, carefully absorbed by me; it echoed my Dubawnt past of crouching in the lee of a large boulder as caribou roamed heedlessly by, including me, it seemed, in the neutrality of their wilderness habitat.

I am fortunate and gratified to share with my family a valued sense of the wild, a reverence for life, and a responsibility to conserve and advocate for protection of endangered habitats and threatened species. Our family is a fourth-generation clan of varying professional and personal persuasions, collectively holding and conserving century-old homestead lands in the Gallatin River valley of southwestern Montana. It is a winter refuge for elk, a seasonal range for sandhill cranes, and a protected natural habitat for bear, wolf, deer, moose, coyote, eagle, hawk, waterfowl, and rainbow trout. And it is my spiritual link, backward in time to that remarkable Dubawnt journey and forward through now, to the future, in the struggle to slow and modify the onslaught of growth, development, and energy exploitation on what remains of the fragile boundaries to the natural and the wild.

Even after these many years, I grieve Art Moffatt's death. He was more than my mentor; he was perhaps a second father even though he was only fourteen years older than I. His pacifism, his principled lifestyle, and his view of the world, natural and international, opened my mind, challenged my thoughts, and gave me insight and courage to pursue my own dreams.

I wonder what would have been the future had he survived the Dubawnt and fully developed professionally as an outdoor writer and voice for wild spaces, indigenous peoples, habitat protection, and restraint in Arctic resource development. I believe his impact on our awareness and understanding of the Barrens would have been profound. How might we have better valued the vastness and uniqueness of that ecosystem? How different our understanding and vision of the far north might be today had our Dubawnt adventure ended in celebration instead of tragedy?

Certainly, we would be better informed, perhaps more compassionate in causes of peace, and probably more courageous in advocating to protect and conserve our northern heritage.

NOTES

1. Andrew Macdonald and James Murphy, "Moffatt, Myth & Mysticism," *Che-Mun,* Spring 1996, p. 5.

2. Bob Thum, in Charlie Mahler, "Down a Dead Man's River," Canoeing.com, *Advanced Paddler,* 2009, p. 2.

3. *Che-Mun,* Spring 1996, p. 5.

4. Book Review, *Appalachia Journal,* December 15, 1996.

5. B. Worthington-Roberts, PhD, University of Washington School of Medicine, personal communication, May 2011.

6. See recipe in the chapter "Getting Started."

7. J. W. Davidson and John Rugge, *The Complete Wilderness Paddler* (New York: Vintage Books, 1975), p. 54; O. Ross McIntyre, *Paddle Beads* (Lyme, N.H.: Graybooks, 2010), p. 121.

8. Tom Bose, in Charlie Mahler, "Down a Dead Man's River," Canoeing .com, *Advanced Paddler,* 2009, p. 5.

9. George Luste, commentary in George Grinnell, *A Death on the Barrens* (Toronto: Northern Books, 1996), p. 281.

10. Larry Osgood, personal communication, February 1996.

11. George Grinnell, *A Death on the Barrens* (Toronto: Northern Books, 1996), p. 50.

12. Art Moffatt's journal, provided by the Rauner Library, Dartmouth College, with permission from Creigh Moffatt.

13. Grinnell, *A Death on the Barrens,* p. 175.

14. Ibid., p. 11.

15. Ibid., p. 49.

16. Ibid., p. 10.

17. Ibid., p. 50.

18. Ibid.

19. Ibid.

20. Ibid., p. 176.

21. Ibid.

22. Luste, commentary in *A Death on the Barrens,* p. 288.

23. Grinnell, *A Death on the Barrens,* p. 164; Fay Franck, personal communication, October 2010.

24. Grinnell, *A Death on the Barrens,* p. 53.

25. Ibid., p. 164.

26. Bruce LeFavour, personal communication, November 6, 2010.

27. George Grinnell, "Art Moffatt's Wilderness Way to Enlightenment," *Canoe,* July 1988, p. 21.

28. Grinnell, *A Death on the Barrens,* p. 139.

29. Ibid., pp. 140–41.

30. Art Moffatt's journal.

31. Grinnell, *A Death on the Barrens,* p. 178.

32. Ibid., p. 178–79.

33. Ibid., p. 179.

34. Luste, commentary in *A Death on the Barrens,* p. 301.

35. Ibid., p. 299.

36. Thum, in "Down a Dead Man's River," p. 6.

37. Luste, commentary in *A Death on the Barrens,* p. 282.

38. Macdonald and Murphy, "Moffatt, Myth & Mysticism," p. 5.

39. Albert Schweitzer, *Out of My Life and Thought,* trans. A. B. Lemke (New York: Henry Holt, 1933, 1949), p. 155, 1990.

40. Ibid., p. 158.

APPENDIX: NONTRAVEL DAYS

DATE	WEATHER	REMARKS
30 Jun	wind, cloudy, hot	AM delay waiting for paddles; PM wind-bound, 2'–3' waves
1 Jul	wind, cloudy	wind-bound, 3'–4' waves
2 Jul	wind, warm	AM left camp, increasing seas forced return to camp; evening calm, paddled 8 mi. after dinner before beaching on rough, windy shore
8 Jul	cloudy, cool, wind	rest after several days of portaging
11 Jul	clear, warm	AM photography, PM travel
12 Jul	clear	AM photography, PM travel
15 Jul	overcast, showers, warm	rest day
22 Jul	wind, overcast	wind-bound, photography
23 Jul	wind, rain PM	wind-bound, photography (birds)
24 Jul	wind, cold, showers	wind-bound
25 Jul	wind, cold	wind-bound all day; left camp 10 PM; paddled until 1:30 AM
27 Jul	overcast, rain	traveled only about two hours

DATE	WEATHER	REMARKS
31 Jul	wind, cold (47F)	wind-bound
2 Aug	wind, rain	wind-bound
3 Aug	wind, rain, cold	wind-bound
5 Aug	wind, overcast, cold (45F)	wind-bound, caribou hunt
11 Aug	partly cloudy, showers PM	photography (duck hawks), caribou hunt
12 Aug	rain	
16 Aug	rain	Nicholson Rapids
17 Aug	rain	Nicholson Rapids
18 Aug	rain	Nicholson Rapids
20 Aug	wind	wind-bound, caribou hunt
27 Aug	clear, cool	rest
29 Aug	clear, wind, warm	rest, built cairn
1 Sept	rain, wind, cold	tent-bound
2 Sept	rain, wind, cold	tent-bound
3 Sept	rain, wind, cold	tent-bound
8 Sept	rain, snow	tent-bound, collecting artifacts
9 Sept	rain, snow	storm-bound
10 Sept	rain, snow, squalls	storm-bound

GLOSSARY

Bull dog A large biting fly.

Cairn A pile of rocks, often pyramidal, sometimes used as a trail marker.

Chain Surveyor's measure of length, approximately sixty-six feet.

Char A fish of the genus *Salvelinus,* related to the trout.

Coaming A raised frame of wood around the sides of a boat or opening on the deck of a boat to prevent water coming aboard.

Current V A current pattern between rocks or other obstructions in swift water, usually marking a clear path between the obstacles.

Dare Devil A metal fishing lure.

Esker A narrow ridge, often sinuous, composed of sand and gravel deposited by a stream flowing beneath or within a glacier or continental ice sheet.

Grayling A fish of the genus *Thymallus* having a small mouth and a large dorsal fin.

Gunnel, Gunwale The upper edge of the side or rail of a small boat.

Hardtack A hard biscuit made with flour and water.

HBC Hudson's Bay Company.

Height-of-land A topographic divide separating watersheds flowing in different directions.

Hornby John Hornby, English-born explorer known for his expeditions in Arctic Canada; starved to death along with two young companions while attempting to winter over in a camp on the Thelon River. Some critics suggest that Hornby was irresponsible in placing the young men in such a perilous, ultimately fatal, situation.

Jaeger A large, aggressive bird of the genus *Stercorarius.*

Johnny cake A traditional travelers' bread made of cornmeal, water/milk, and leavening; baked or fried, often on an open fire.

Kamatik Inuit term for a sledge.

Labrador tea A low-growing evergreen shrub of the genus *Ledum.*

Lichen A complex plant made up of an alga and a fungus growing in symbiotic relationship on various solid surfaces and constituting a major food source for caribou.

Moraine An accumulation of earth materials deposited by a glacier or continental ice sheet, sometimes in the form of a ridge delineating a former ice margin.

Muskeg A swamp or bog formed by the accumulation of decaying plant material.

Peterhead An RCMP patrol boat with a wooden hull approximately forty-five feet in length.

Pothole lake A small lake or pond occupying a roughly circular depression in glaciated terrain, also called a kettle lake.

Ptarmigan A bird of the genus *Lapopus* having feathered feet and plumage that is brown in summer and white in winter.

RCMP Royal Canadian Mounted Police.

SLR Single lens reflex camera.

Tuktu Inuit term for caribou.

Tumpline A strap usually slung across the forehead to support a load carried on the back.

Tump To carry a load using a tumpline.

Tundra A level or undulating treeless plain having a permanently frozen subsoil and supporting low-growing vegetation such as lichens, moss, and stunted shrubs.